AfterWorld

The Divine Comedy of Thomas Buchetta

by Joe Randazzo

A Sprezzatura Book

from New Renaissance Press

Sprezzatura Books
New Renaissance Press
8 Woodside Drive
South Burlington, VT 05403

ISBN 9780970827968

Library of Congress Control Number 2011918210

This book is a work of fiction. Character names and incidents in the plot are products of the author's imagination. Any resemblance to actual events or persons, living or dead, is entirely coincidental.

Covers and author's photograph: Chris Koch

Dedicated to:

Rita Randazzo: Heavenly

Dante Alighieri

Gene Roddenberry

Also by Joe Randazzo

Poetry
Coffee House
His/Hers: Mars and Venus Write Poetry
(with Rita Randazzo)

Novels
Screen
Van Eyck's Secret
See Dick Run: A Grownup's Picture Book
Walking Man

Photodocumentary
Going With the Wind: Carolina in My Mind

ADVANCE COMMENTS FOR *AfterWorld*

Author Joe Randazzo has documented what we all suspected, that Italians are indeed the center of the Universe.

Prince Machiavelli

For an ordinary layman, Mr. Randazzo's character, Thomas Buchetta, shows an inordinately thorough understanding of theology.

Saint Thomas Aquinas

To read Randazzo's *AfterWorld* is to enter the bizarre and disgusting world of a depraved lunatic.

Benito Mussolini

Thomas Buchetta is very sexy. Joe Randazzo must also be very sexy.

Anna Magnani

If Joe Randazzo were my husband, I would have put poison in his wine.

Catherine de Medici
(If you were my wife, I would have drunk it. JR)

There can be no book about Italians, about *my* tribe, without *me* being in it. I did it *my* way. Randazzo did it his way. He did the right thing giving *me* an important role.

Frank Sinatra

Wait until I get my hands on Randazzo!

Giacchino il Strappo

1

"What was that? Where am I?"

Thomas felt a brief second of intense pain and is now dazed and fuzzy. He suddenly sees soft blue and green lights and hears a quiet voice.

"Hello, Thomas Buchetta."

"Yes, who are you?"

"My name is Rose, and I'm your Guide."

"Guide for what?"

"Let me explain what just happened. You were riding in your car and talking to your wife, Cindy, on your cellphone. You didn't see that cement truck pull out in front of you. They should pass a law in Vermont against talking and driving but, of course, that won't help you now. You heard a squeaking sound and asked her what it was. She said she didn't know. Do you remember that?"

"I vaguely remember the sound and seeing a truck, but only for a split second. I don't remember anything else."

"That's because you are now dead. You hit the back end of that truck at seventy miles an hour. You didn't have your seatbelt on, and you went through the windshield into the side of the mixer while it was spinning."

"Dead? How can I be dead if we're having this conversation?"

"It's very complicated, but in time you will understand all. We are having this conversation because our thoughts are combining. All the thoughts you ever had throughout your whole life form the basis of how you will live on afterward. You see, the energy from thoughts never dies. It's electrical energy that lives on in time and space. Your thoughts have a life of their own and can appear and reappear at will anywhere in the Universe. You can control them, and sometimes others try to control them."

"What did you say your name is?"

"Rose."

"Rose, I didn't think it would be like this. When I was a child, I learned in Sunday School that if you led a good life, when you died you would go to Heaven. If you were a rotten turd, you would go to Hell. You mean that I'm in some kind of cyberspace that is no different than my dreams?"

Thomas is uncomfortable. He squirms. Actually, he remembers a time when he was in the third grade and had to go to the bathroom. His teacher was in a very bad mood and yelled at the class for no reason. He was afraid to go ask, so he sat in his chair squirming until the class was over. He then ran as fast as he could, but peed his pants just as he was opening the restroom door.

"You mean this isn't Heaven?"

"We don't use words like Heaven, Hell, Purgatory, Limbo, Nirvana, Happy Hunting Grounds, or whatever. This is the Enlightened EtherWorld. And before we go any further, there is one word that you must never say. I will spell it backward for you: D·O·G. Remember now, when I use the word 'say' or the word 'feel,' you are really *thinking* these things. You do not have the power of speech, and you can no longer *feel* in the physical sense, because you are dead.

"I was a Hungarian Jew, and spoke only Hungarian, Polish, and a little French. You spoke English. That doesn't matter here, because whatever language we used in life, our mental images of water, of children, or of a book or a flower are the same. I know what goes on in your world because here, you continue to learn and expand. So, to get back to my important warning, that D·O·G word is used as an alarm word that activates the entire Sector. It's a sort of panic button, a 911 call, do you understand?"

"Yes."

"Good. If you should use that word, several billion Entities in this and other Sectors will be aroused and further action would be needed. You could wind up in Room 214. I know what you're going to ask: What's in Room 214? I can't tell you now, but we'll get into that later."

"Rose, what is this Sector? Are there other Sectors?"

"We have forever to talk about this. For now, I will let you get accustomed to your new home for a while. Just let your thoughts spin freely. You are in a protected environment, and only positive, nurturing thoughts will be combining with yours."

"You mean there are other thoughts?"

"There are, but not to worry, we'll talk about them later also."

Thomas taps deep into his subconscious, his unconscious, all the people, places, things, thoughts, yearnings that made up his life. They are suddenly accessible to him. If only he could have done this while he was still alive! The Room that Rose has placed him in is very beautiful. All he sees are lights that remind him of the Aurora Borealis. He wonders if he is actually seeing this with a fresh mind, or if he is remembering it. He doesn't recall ever seeing a real Aurora. The colors dance back and forth across his mind like a huge 180-degree panoramic movie screen. He feels at total peace for the first time in his existence. After a long while, Rose appears next to him and gently brings him back to the present.

"Thomas, this is a place you can return to any time you want. All external energy is filtered out. This is Room TP, Total Peace."

"How many other Sectors are there, Rose?"

"Sector A is closest to Room 214. In it are people like Mother Teresa; Albert Schweitzer; Joan of Arc; Rabbi Alexander Goode, Reverends George L. Fox and Clark V. Poling, and Father John P. Washington, the Four Chaplains on the World War II ship *U.S.A.T. Dorchester* who gave up their life vests so other sailors would live; Saint Francis; Anne Frank; and thousands of others like them. This Sector contains saintly people. By the way, Reverend Fox was from your home state of Vermont.

"Sector B is for very good people who went through life helping others: Red Cross volunteers, nurses, teachers, and so forth."

"What Sector are you from, Rose?"

"I'm from Sector B. It's standard procedure for all Initiates in Sector C to have Guides from Sector B. Sector C is the largest of all, and contains the ordinary people who have done more Good than Evil. Sector C is interesting because it's a great blending. You can never change Sectors at your whim. That's decided by Room 214. You can grow and learn, however, in the AfterWorld, and mix with those in any Sector if you are accompanied by your Guide. No one really pays any attention to where you are from, and in most cases they don't even know.

"There are many Sectors, A through Z, AA through ZZ, and numbers 1 to 100,000. I'm telling you some of them. Sector R is full of rich people like the Rockefellers, Vanderbilts, Goulds, Firestones, Fords, and politicians like Nixon and Johnson. They didn't commit heinous crimes themselves, but their decisions affected the lives of millions of people, many of whom died from hunger, from war, or had their homes repossessed, or perished because they couldn't afford medical care. All because of the actions of beings in Sector R.

"This group is just above Sector T, the Treachery Sector. It's in the NetherWorld. The EtherWorld goes up through Sector E, and the NetherWorld starts at Sector F, a very bad place. There are Rooms within each Sector both here and in the NetherWorld. It can get confusing, because there are the same letters in both Worlds, but very different inhabitants.

"Room S is a sealed Room that contains Evil life forms that are unknown to Humans. Think of it as a ten-foot-diameter steel ball with a peanut-sized center. All the Beings are in the center, and the mass of the steel ball is needed to contain them. This is the only Room in the EtherWorld with Evil Beings. Only Room 214 knows who or what is in there and how they got there, and he doesn't want them to fall into NetherWorld hands. People of like mind, of shared interests or professions, will form Rooms within each Sector."

"Rose, is the Treachery Sector truly Evil?"

"Thomas, did you ever see the movie *Lord of the Rings*?"

"Yes, I did."

"Do you remember the dark, fiery world of Mordor? Have you ever read Dante's 'Inferno'? He talks about the circles of hell. The first circle is Limbo, the second is Lust, the third is Gluttony, the fourth is Greed, the fifth Anger, sixth is Heresy, seventh is Violence, eighth is Fraud, and the ninth, Treachery. The Treachery Sector is just like Mordor. By the way, do you notice how Fraud is in the next to worst circle? There are some people in your country from Wall Street who are in for a surprise."

"Surprise, how? What do you mean? If they can only relive their thoughts, how can they be surprised?"

Rose grabs Thomas and travels with him past a blur of light, sound, and very confusing images to Sector T, the Treachery Sector in the NetherWorld. They are cloaked and will remain undetected for seven micro-clocks, enough time for Rose to educate Thomas. She puts two powerful filters in place so he can't see the full horrors.

"Thomas, this Sector was renamed very recently in honor of Dante's ninth circle. Here is a partial list of the inhabitants and the reason they are here."

Mao Ze-Dong	killed	60,000,000	people
Josef Stalin		20,000,000	
Adolph Hitler		12,000,000	
Pol Pot		1,700,000	
Kim Il Sung		1,600,000	
Saddam Hussein		500,000	
Benito Mussolini		300,000	
Osama Bin Laden		3,500	

"Also in Sector T are thousands of murderers such as Attila the Hun, Maximilien Robespierre, Idi Amin Dada, Ivan IV of Russia, Timothy McVeigh, Jack the Ripper. You get the idea."

"Why are they all in the T Sector if their thoughts want to take them somewhere else?"

"Occasionally, they...how can I say this in terms you will understand...they escape across the border into a more pleasant world, mostly of childhood memories. But they are quickly thrown back to Sector T by the thoughts of so many others who have been harmed by them. They can never obtain permanent entry into the EtherWorld without permission of Room 214. Occasionally, the T Beings pool their thoughts and do harm to others."

Thomas remembers fear. "Do you mean that Evil still exists here?"

"Absolutely. The battle of Good and Evil goes on here just as it did in our old World."

"What was your World like, Rose? What was your full name, and how did you die?"

"Let's not talk about me yet."

"Yes, I want to know."

"My full name is Rose von Kolisch, and I died in a concentration camp during the Holocaust in 1944."

"So how can you even look at Adolph Hitler?"

"You will learn that you can use your thoughts to punish people. You may know that Hitler had only one ball. I can tell you that it has been cut off 12,000,000 times. Now that the descendants of Holocaust victims are also dying, the count will probably double. The energy is so strong, they just pull him out of the T Sector and work him over."

"Will the pain ever stop for him?"

"Possibly, but it will take a long time. That is what people on Earth describe as 'Hell.' In the 65 years since the war ended, only two people have forgiven him. So, you can do the math to see how long he will stay in Sector T. Just remember one important thing, Thomas. If you are ever assaulted by negative thoughts, or if souls try to do you harm, just remember Room TP, and you will be instantly transported back to that place. 214 has never failed to grant that. That Room is strictly off limits to everyone else, except me, your Guide."

"Thank you, Rose. I'm feeling very overwhelmed, and I'd like to go there now."

Thomas returns to Room TP and sits alone in the Aurora Panorama. The colors are the same, but this time many beautiful memories of his life slowly combine with the colors. He remembers his sixth birthday and the Lionel train set his parents gave him for Christmas. He remembers pushing his baby brother in the backyard swing. He remembers one afternoon when his agent called to tell Thomas he had sold his first novel. He remembers the first time he saw the ocean, the first time he ate a pizza, and the first time he made love. He remembers how, at age 13, he helped his father paint the house. He fearlessly climbed the ladder to paint the second-story trim. He was rewarded with a gas-powered model airplane. He remembers winning an award in the eighth grade for the highest score on the Regents Exam. He lingers in this space, mostly remembering childhood and early adolescence, happy with his life. He is anxious to resume his orientation. Rose knows this and she is ready to show him his new Universe.

★

"Thomas, think of wandering into stores, the same way that you would go shopping in a European city. Have you ever been to Europe?"

"Oh yes, several times."

"Good, so you know that the European cities, especially the smaller ones, are very different from the American. They don't have huge box stores, but many small shops. A French housewife will do her shopping daily and go to as many as seven or more places to buy bread, fish, vegetables, or whatever. There are specialty shops for all kinds of things. The same is true here. These aren't Sectors, but *Rooms* for people of like mind. There are millions of them. For instance, there are thousands for Beings who used to practice law. There are Rooms full of lawyers. They used to try cases, but now they're just trying. I used to be a nurse in a children's hospital in Budapest, so I love to visit some of the nurses' Rooms. There's a Room for blondes, a Room for people who liked to listen to Luciano Pavarotti. There's a Room for people who owned velvet paintings of Elvis. There are Rooms for writers like yourself. Actually, there are about 20,000 Rooms for writers. I see you wrote novels."

"Yes, but my first two books bombed. They sold very badly, and I didn't even make my advance. I had to go to work at Home Depot because no one else was hiring out-of-work writers. I had just finished my third book when I hit that cement truck."

Thomas likes Rose and wonders if they will be traveling companions. He remembers his sexual feelings. Actually, he is tormented by a very strong attraction to Rose and doesn't know what to do about it. Rose continues with the orientation.

"Thomas, Sentient Beings, other than Humans, make up the vast majority of energy in the Universe. Right now you have only a vague sense of their existence, but this will change."

Thomas asks, "What was *that* energy?"

"That was a cat."

"A cat! You mean there are cats here? Why should they be allowed to mix with higher life forms? I hate cats. They were always digging and crapping in my garden. They ruined some tomatoes, so I squirted them with my hose."

"Thomas, see if you can understand this: *Joiw/sklw/mnvop/wyeuw/asqoxcv/wobabbariba.*"

"I don't know what that means."

"That, Mr. Hotshot, is the very roughest translation of speech from a Sentient Being in another Galaxy. They often pass through, but since all their experience and mental images are different from yours, there can be no communication until Room 214 translates it.

"I know your concerns are important to you, but let me give you a little perspective here. As you probably know, Earth is part of the Milky Way Galaxy. There are 400 billion stars in our Galaxy. Now, if they all have about the same number of planets as our Sun, that's close to four trillion planets in the Milky Way alone. There are over 500 billion Galaxies in the Universe. Do you have any idea how many of them have life on them? Do the math and stop being a jerk. You are just not that important."

"Great, thanks for making me feel so special."

"There's more. Do you remember what a slug looks like?"

"Yes."

"Are they a lower life form than a Human?"

"Yes. When I caught them trying to eat my tomatoes, I poured beer on them. I liked to watch them squirm and dissolve."

"Thomas, you need a lot of work. Look here, Mr. Higher Life Form, there are Sentient Beings in the Universe who are as far above us as we are above that slug. And there are still others that are as far above the first group of Sentient Beings. Do you get the idea? In some Sectors, we are no more than germs. So go easy on that cat. He knows much more about being a cat than you did about being a Human."

"How do you know all this? Where do you get your information?"

"From Room 214."

"Is that G...."

"DON'T SAY THE WORD!"

"I don't get it, Rose. Someone had to create all this. It couldn't have come from nothing."

"Why not?"

"Because everything has to have a beginning."

"Your *mind* tells you that everything has to have a beginning."

"Bullshit! Not just *my* mind, all the great astronomers and scientists on Earth say the Universe started with a grand explosion, the Big Bang from something the size of a pea. Theologians like Aquinas talk about a Prime Mover who made the pea."

Rose increases her intensity. "Did those scientists and theologians ever mention Parallel Universes? Did they ever mention Universes existing in other dimensions? Did they mention that there's a whole can of peas in your terrestrial supermarket, and that there's a whole aisle of different kinds of peas in the supermarket? Can you grasp the idea that the Universe always existed and that there is more than one Universe?"

"They had to have a beginning."

"Fine, Thomas, we'll discuss this later, right now we have to..."

Thomas sees a female body in a thin veil drift by. She floats away like a jellyfish in a strong current. (Thomas was prone to bad metaphors. That's why his first two books didn't do that well.)

"Who was that?"

"That was Salome from Room W."

"What is Room W?"

"Room W is where all the great beauties of the world hang out, but you absolutely shouldn't go in there."

"Rose, who is in the Room?"

"Here's a partial list."

Marilyn Monroe
Jayne Mansfield
Elizabeth Taylor
Lena Horne
Mae West
Josephine Baker
Cleopatra
Venus
Aphrodite
Delilah

Salome

Queen Nefertiti

Helen of Troy

Xi Shi, Wang Zhaojun, Diaochan, Yang Guifei: the Four Great Beauties of China

"You get the idea, but again I strongly caution you against entering. You're not ready."

Thomas remembers when he was fourteen years old. He and two friends lied about their age and went to see an X-rated movie at the Majestic. It was an old theater that showed a sleazy movie every Thursday afternoon. The rest of the week it was strictly family fare. At that time Burlington, Vermont was a rather stodgy New England city, but the townsfolk looked the other way. Eventually the Majestic burned down and a Dick's Sporting Goods now stands in the same spot. The point of all this is that the only movies Thomas wanted to see were the ones he was not allowed to see.

He enters Room W and takes a stroll down a long corridor with beaded curtains on either side. There is the aroma of incense, and laughter from female voices. On either side of the corridor are many compartments, and each one has a different beauty who walks up to the beaded curtain to welcome him. As he passes one, he hears two women arguing. He separates the curtain and looks inside. In the compartment are Cleopatra and Elizabeth Taylor, who are shouting at each other.

"Hey, the two of you look exactly alike."

Elizabeth Taylor speaks, "You are a moron. We look alike to you because the only time you saw Cleopatra was in the movies, and I played her. In actuality she was a little runt. Let me give you the straight skinny here, or is it the straight fat. The real Cleopatra, this slut, had a large nose, her eyes were too close together, and her hair was all matted from not being washed for weeks on end. She slathered perfume all over herself to hide the stink."

"Runt, stink, is that so, Elizabeth. I brought the Roman Empire to its knees, and I had the real Marc Antony, not some actor. What do you have to show for your life, Richard Burton and Eddie Fisher? How many husbands did you have, nine?"

"None of them would have looked twice at a runt like you. You were only five feet tall and plump as a watermelon."

"You believe your own hype, you overblown egomaniac. Your press clippings list you at five-foot-four, but that's in your high heels. You were no taller than five-foot-two yourself, and for a while there you looked more like a blimp than a watermelon. *The Taming of the Shrew* was the only film you could do justice to. I had an entire country throwing flowers at my feet, and I didn't need a press agent to inflate my worth. We'll just see who gives Thomas a better time."

"Go play in the sand. You have absolutely no class."

They are interrupted by two other Beings who are across the corridor.

"Hello, Tommy, I'm Marilyn. Say, you're cute! Did you just get here? This is my friend Jayne. We have nothing on underneath these togas. We'll just slip them off and cuddle up to you."

Jayne says, "Those exotic British and Egyptian eyes are okay, I guess, but wouldn't you rather enjoy some proven American pulchritude? Come on, follow us."

Thomas follows them into their space.

"This is more like it!"

Suddenly Thomas is grabbed by a cloaked female and yanked out of Room W before he can do anything.

2.

"Rohhhhhhhhhhhhhhhhhhhhhhhhhhhhhhhhhhhhhhze!"

"Rohhhhhhhhhhhhhhhhhhhhhhhhhhhhhhhhhhhhhhze!"

"Rohhhhhhhhhhhhhhhhhhhhhhhhhhhhhhhhhhhhhhze!"

"What?"

"Where am I?"

"You were placed in a Containment Room. You can send thoughts but can't receive them. I had to go to Room 214 to bail you out. I told you not to go in there, and you ignored me. The Virgin Mary is chaperone of Room W, and she has this thing about sex. Thomas, don't touch me there! Is that all you think about?"

"I'm sorry, but I want to get to know you better."

"There is a no-sex rule between Initiates and Guides. Perhaps later. Come here, I want to show you something."

Rose takes Thomas out of the Containment Room to the edge of dark matter. Thomas remembers a blank movie screen just before the picture started. All of a sudden, a swirling mass of light, strange music, and lilting sounds appear in motion from right to left. It lasts for about fifty Earth-minutes and was the best light show he had ever seen.

"What was that?"

"That was a Swirl, 10,000 Sentient Beings all having sex with each other at the same time. There are Ancient Greeks, Victorian Ladies, Neanderthals, Beings from planets around the stars Arcturus and Betelgeuse, the entire cast of the Folies Bergere Paris, Adonis, Lord Byron, Hercules, Gary Cooper, yum, and many more. After a while, you won't want to waste time in Room W. I'm invited to a Swirl tomorrow, so I won't see you for a few weeks."

"A few *weeks*?"

"You're dead, remember. Things aren't the same here."

"When will I be invited to a Swirl?"

"I'm not satisfied with the pace of your orientation, so I thought I'd offer this enticement, this view of a Swirl to keep you focused. You will be invited when you pass your tests."

"What tests?"

"The testing committee will contact you while I'm away. Don't forget about Room Total Peace. It will do you good to wander about Sector C for a while. Try entering Rooms with which you have some familiarity. Unknowns may be too much for you to handle. You will not be able to visit other Sectors just yet. See you in two weeks, as you used to measure time."

"Aw, Rose, take me with you. Can't you make an exception just this once?"

"No, see you in two weeks."

"Rose, I have one more question before you go. Is there a directory of all the Rooms in Sector C, some sort of a divine Excel sheet?"

"Yes, there is. It's in Room L, but you won't be able to read but a few of them. Some titles will just be gibberish. The Rooms are listed but not *what or who* is in them. Best to enter those that you recognize by the names."

Thomas decides to visit Room L and check the writers' Rooms. He travels to one devoted to American short story writers. All the greats are sitting before him in a huge smoking club. Pipe tobacco smoke from Turkey and America fills the air, and the authors are reading newspapers.

"Greetings, Thomas, my name is Frank Stockton. I died in 1902."

"I know your work, Mr. Stockton. You wrote 'The Lady or the Tiger,' about a man who was punished for loving the King's daughter. He was taken to an arena and put before two doors. Behind one was a vicious, hungry tiger, and behind the other was a gorgeous lady who he could marry. The Princess was in the arena crowd and pointed him toward the door on the right. Your story ends just as he was opening that door. I always wanted to know which was behind the door, the lady or the tiger?"

Frank Stockton has an amused expression on his face.

"That's 17,658,232 times I've been asked the same question. I will give you the answer I gave all the others. There is nothing behind that door. Whatever is in the reader's mind, that is what he places in the room. Is the glass half empty or half full?"

"Shit!" Thomas raises his voice and the writers look up from their reading.

"That's a cop-out. It reminds me of the last episode of *The Sopranos*. You must know what you intended."

"Thomas, what did you think was behind the door?"

"I thought it was the tiger because the Princess you wrote about was somewhat cruel, so she was probably jealous."

"Then that is your reality."

"Cop-out!"

Thomas leaves the American short story writers Room and has an exciting thought. Now he can explore all the great mysteries and find out what the truth is. Did Lee Harvey Oswald act alone? Who built Stonehenge? Do things disappear in the Bermuda Triangle? Was there ancient life on Mars? Was there an Atlantis? Was Jack the Ripper a member of the royal family? Who killed Marilyn Monroe? *I should have asked her when I was in Room W, but that was the furthest thing from my mind.*

★

The testing committee contacts Thomas, and he is summoned to Room TR, which is the Sector C Initiates Testing and Training Center. There are rows of desks that remind him of a large lecture hall at MIT. He sits in the last row and is approached by a proctor who hands him an answer sheet and a special pencil. A voice booms from a hidden loudspeaker.

"Please put on the headphones that you see on top of your desk. Your tests have been individualized and will relate to your own experiences during the first few months you have been with us. The questions will be asked aloud, and you will pencil in the correct answer next to the blank space by each number. In some cases there are multiple-choice questions. Fill in the small box next to the letter, A, B, C, D, or E, that you think is correct. Make sure your marks are nice and dark. As you can see, there is a tube attached to the left side of your headset. This is a small microphone. If you have any questions, please speak softly so you don't disturb the Being next to you. This test will last approximately twenty minutes. There will be a ten-minute break followed by another twenty-minute test. We will begin now."

"This is bullshit," Thomas says out loud. The proctor walks over to his desk and asks him if there's a problem, but Thomas just stares at the answer sheet. He hears the first question over the headphones.

"What is in Room S?"

Thomas doesn't write the answer and just sits there with his arms folded. The second question is:

"What is your Guide's full name?"

He thinks *Rose von something or other* but doesn't remember.

"This is bullshit," he says again. The proctor asks him why he isn't writing anything down.

"Because this test is totally useless. Why do I have to answer these stupid questions?"

"Because you have to prove you know the answers before you can be Certified."

"Certified? Why do I want to get Certified?"

"You can't attend a Swirl or ride the SlingShot unless you're Certified."

"I know what a Swirl is, but what the hell is a SlingShot, and why do I want to ride it?"

"The SlingShot takes you to other Galaxies. If you pass all your tests, you will be granted Explorer status and be able to observe and eventually mix with other Sentient Beings in faraway Galaxies."

"Who cares? I'm out of here. I'll just wander around the Rooms. The hell with the Swirl! I'll find a Room where I can find a little piece of..."

"That's your choice, Thomas, and it may do for a while, but you will quickly see that you need to expand and grow beyond this Sector."

Thomas leaves Room TR and wanders around aimlessly. He sees a new Mercedes convertible drive by with a middle-aged woman at the wheel.

"Cars? There are cars up here?" he says out loud. The driver sees him and stops. There isn't a road surface, and the car is just floating in space.

"Hi there, want to go for a ride? Hop in."

Thomas sees that it's a brand new car, burgundy red with SatNav GPS. He hears music for the first time in the AfterWorld, a Jimi Hendrix song his father used to play.

"Where did you get this car?" he asks the woman.

"Well, I was singing one of my songs, 'Oh Lord won't you buy me a Mercedes Benz, my friends all drive Porsches, I must make amends. Worked hard all my lifetime, no help from my friends, so oh Lord won't you buy me a Mercedes Benz.' And there it was, man. Don't need the GPS, though."

"I know who you are, I recognize your voice. You're Janis Joplin."

Thomas knows all about Janis since she was his father's favorite singer. He used to play her records constantly and drove his mother crazy. His father was born the same year as Janis, 1943. Thomas was born the same year Janis died, 1970. When he had a band in college, there was a singer who sounded like Janis, and they used to play Big Brother and the Holding Company songs. But now Janis is much older than he could have imagined.

"Thomas, you're good, man. Most people don't recognize me. I used computer modeling to age myself. When I rode around the way I was, with my little sunglasses, I was always bothered by people wanting autographs. When I go to my Room, I change back."

"You can do that, change your appearance at will?"

"Sure. How are you doing with your Certification?"

"I walked out. That test was bullshit."

"You need to be Certified, man, it's really cool. You can do some neat shit. That SlingShot is beyond groovy, it's totally awesome. Hey, let's go to my Room and I'll show you around. Do you play?"

"Guitar and sax. Not bad on the guitar, but a real good horn, even recorded some."

"Great, we have all kinds of instruments in Room 27. There's a brand new Mark IV Selmer tenor that's got your name on it."

Thomas and Janis enter Room 27, and she changes back to the way she looked when she died. There are many others in the Room.

"Thomas, this is a special place. Everyone in this room is a musician or singer who died at age twenty-seven. Let me introduce you to some of them. Hey gang, this is Thomas, he blows sax. This is Robert Johnson and Brian Jones. Here's my new special friend. Hey, Amy, come and meet Thomas. Thomas, this is Amy Winehouse. Amy is already Certified. You know some of these guys, Jimi Hendrix, Jim Morrison, Kurt Cobain. Hey guys, introduce yourselves and tell Thomas what group you were in. This is cool."

Roger Lee Durham from Bloodstone
Rudy Lewis, the Drifters
Alan Wilson, Canned Heat
Pete Ham, Badfinger
Jacob Miller, Inner Circle
Jean-Michael Basquiat, Gray
Maria Serrano Serrano, Passion Fruit
Pete de Freitas, Echo and the Bunnymen
Pigpen McKernan, The Grateful Dead

Janis says, "You gotta admit, hon, Pigpen's band has the best name up here."

Jimi Hendrix grabs his left-handed Strat and plays "All Along the Watchtower." The notes flow like water over flat stones. Thomas grabs the Selmer Mark IV and fills in some riffs. Janis and Amy sing an unbelievably great dissonant harmony with Jimi.

"Thomas, we all make music together. Man, I wish I was a record producer on Earth with this talent. We do things we never did before. People who never met until they came here are jamming together. We have a complete library of our music."

Janis opens the door to a huge room full of CDs. "The CDs are just symbolic, because the energy is stored in all our consciousnesses. But look at the titles."

Thomas is like the proverbial kid in a candy store as he scans the shelves. He sees the album titles and musicians on the albums:

Terra Nova
>Robert Johnson
>Brian Jones
>Nat Jaffe
>Rudy Lewis
>Roger Lee Durham

Twice is Not Enough
>Janis Joplin
>Kurt Cobain
>Pete Ham
>Rudy Lewis

Beware the Ninth Circle
>Amy Winehouse
>Linda Jones
>Dickie Pride
>Dyke Christian

"Hey man, you should get Certified. There's a planet in the Sombrero Galaxy called DeJive that's nothing but music. You should hear the stuff they play. There's an ocean harp that is fed by twenty Beings pouring water down solid silver pipes. The player raises and lowers the pipes. The instrument is four hundred feet long. There's another that is played by a Being with seven 'hands,' as we would call them. It's a stringed instrument, but all the strings are bent around soundboards of exotic material. He starts with just one hand, but by the time he's finished, all seven are going wild. He's part of a four-piece combo that includes the ocean harp, a percussionist who uses his seven hands like you have never seen, beating on all sorts of shit, and some kind of keyboard that sounds like a choir. If you go to another part of DeJive, there is a totally different culture with other weird instruments."

"I'm confused, Janis. Are these Beings alive or are they dead?"

"They're dead, man, same as us, but they jam just like we do."

Thomas goes back to Room TR and gets special permission to finish his test. He remembers Rose's last name, von Kolisch. He passes with honors.

★

"Helloooooooo Thomas," Rose says as she spins to a stop in front of him.

"You look and sound very happy, Rose."

Rose is smiling, but she quickly tries to change the subject.

"I see you passed your tests. This is very good."

"How was your Swirl?"

"Thomas, you have only three more tests before you become Certified, and I'm very proud of you."

"How was your Swirl?"

"Thomas, up here we don't kiss and tell. Everyone loves everyone, but the details are strictly private."

"So how come I was rousted out of Room W?"

"Because you're still an Initiate, and I told you it was a sensitive area."

"So can we now get on with my orientation?"

"Don't be so impatient. I may have done you a disservice showing you that Swirl. Those pleasures are the most basic, but there will be others much more satisfying. You were shown the Swirl because that is now closest to your understanding, which is primitive. I'm not trying to put you down, but after a while you will equally embrace other pleasures."

"I can't get no satisfaction. I can't get no reaction, though I try, yes I try."

"Very funny, Thomas. Let's go to Room L and study some of the undecipherable Room names."

As Rose and Thomas drift toward Room L, Thomas hears a conversation:

So I says to him, I says,
enough already with my daughter.
So he says to me, he says,
we did nothin'.
So I grabbed him and I says,
so how come she's pregnant?
So he says to me, he says,
I used a condom.
So I says to him, I says,
I thought you said you did nothin'.
So he runs to his car,
so help me Gina, he runs to his car
the coward,
and leaves rubber all over the street.
Wait until I tell my husband.

"Rose, that's a strange blending of thoughts that I haven't heard before."

"Oh nuts, that's my fault. I'm supposed to filter these out."

"What are these?"

"Thomas, it gets complicated. You see, those weren't thoughts from Beings in this space. The thoughts *are* in this space, but they didn't *originate* in this space. What you just heard is a cellphone conversation taking place in New Jersey, in the U.S.A. Before the age of wireless telephones, radios, televisions, cellphones, texting devices, and wireless computers, all electrical energy was generated by us and by the other Sentient Beings. So all the energy from these communications, as well as those from other worlds, are mixing with our thoughts. That is, they have the potential to mix with our thoughts. It's very easy after a short while to identify them. We have no ability to return the thoughts or interfere with the devices, only to receive them."

"So, when Humans pray for something to happen, there really isn't any action taken by Beings in these Sectors, or by Room 214." Thomas is searching for answers.

"It does happen sometimes, but it takes billions of thoughts directed to the same place, and it must be approved by Room 214. I need a refresher course because of all these new electronic devices. There are strange words that I've never heard before, words like *cyberbullying*, *noob*, *woot*, *sexting*, *muffintop*, *meep*. And there are so many new abbreviations that people are using in texting. I heard some the other day and wrote them down, but I don't know what they mean."

"You mean you *remembered* them. Rose, you don't have to use the image anymore of writing them down. I know they're in your consciousness."

"Great, Thomas, here's what I remember."

Rose supplies the abbreviation, and Thomas instantly tells her the meanings:

1174	nude club
182	I hate you
2BZ4UQT	Too busy for you cutey
8	Oral sex
AFT	About fucking time
AYSOS	Are you stupid or something
BAC	Bad ass chick
BAMF	Bad ass mother fucker
BFD	Big fucking deal

"That's amazing, Thomas. Your knowledge of modern urban communications is vast."

"Thank you, Rose, but that's just some of them through the letter B. As you can see, communications have changed somewhat since Jane Austin's day."

"It makes me sad, Thomas. Now people Tweet, Twitter, Text, and send nude photos of themselves back and forth via cellphone. As you say, in Jane Austin's time they used quill pens and seldom wrote a bad word. Thomas, we could use you at our next communications meeting to help educate us in this new language. How did you learn so much about it?"

"Research for my last novel."

Thomas accompanies Rose to the next communications meeting, and becomes the first non-Certified Initiate ever to teach at an advanced briefing. He instantly becomes the recognized expert in modern communications. Rose is instructed not to filter out any of the messages that come from Earth. Thomas is now highly motivated and learns quickly. As Amy Winehouse did, he earns his Certification in near record time.

"Congratulations, Thomas, you are now Certified."

"Rose, when is the next Swirl, and are you going?"

"Fuhgeddaboudit."

3

"Rose, now that I'm Certified, how long are you going to be my Guide?"

"You're just getting started. Certification is only one of the five steps for which Initiates need the presence of a Guide. The five steps are:
1 – Certification
2 – Exploration
3 – Sentient Reciprocity
4 – Universal Awareness
5 – Enlightenment
"How long the process takes is up to you. A few Beings in Sector A have reached Enlightenment in five days. For others, it took 150 years. There is no *average* time because no such records are kept."

Thomas is pleased and has many questions for Rose. He holds them because much has happened and he needs to check into Room TP to collect himself. He welcomes the sight of the Aurora Panorama. Thomas concentrates on his life on Earth, his plans, and his unfulfilled dreams.

Rose is summoned by Room 214 and is given special instructions.

"Thomas, there is something we have to talk about. Since you have been here you have not exhibited any empathy for other Beings. We appreciate what you have done with new communications, but 214 is troubled by your lack of caring for others. They feel that your offer of help was more ambition than caring. You have been directed to appear in Room HS."

"What is Room HS?"

"Room Head Shrink. There's a panel of experts that wants to evaluate you. HS recommendations are very important, so please don't overreact or show that you have a chip on your shoulder. I know you're not happy about this, and neither am I, but there you have it."

Thomas glides to Room HS and is greeted by a receptionist named Freida. She has teased blonde hair about nine inches above the top of her head, and she speaks with a decidedly New York City accent.

"Welcome, Thomas Buchetta, you can sit dere and wait if you wanna. What is your date of birth, please?

"March 3, 1970."

"Da doctors will see you in a few minutes. Dere's some magazines on the table if youse would like to read dem."

On the table are magazines in German from Vienna dated 1906, and an *Atlantic Monthly* from 1923.

"You can come in now." Freida escorts Thomas to a medium-sized room. There's a beige velvet couch with a built-in cylindrically shaped pillow. It is brand new, and it appears that he is the first to use it. There are three men sitting in carved wood and leather chairs surrounding him, and he is very nervous.

They introduce themselves:
"I'm Carl Jung."
"I'm Alfred Adler."
"And I'm Sigmund Freud."

Freud tells Thomas he is here because on his medical record there's mention of him squirting cats with his hose, and pouring beer on slugs while he watched them squirm and dissolve. It also states in his history that he seems to have a preoccupation with sex, and he was thrown out of Room W by the Virgin Mary.

Adler asks the first question. "Thomas, vas dot goot beer zat you poured on zee slugs, Wertzberger, perhaps?"

"No, it was Budweiser."

"Ach! No goot," Jung exclaimed. All at the same time, they wrote negative notes in their journals.

Adler continues: "Tell us about your childhood, all zee goot stuff, especially zee sexy parts. Vare vas you born? Did you masturbate often?   Did anyone ever catch you masturbating?"

Thomas refuses to discuss his early childhood.

Freud asks him why he became a writer when he had studied to become an engineer at MIT.

"I became an electrical engineer because my father is an electrical engineer. And like my father, I went to work at IBM. I hated it and became a writer instead. My father wouldn't speak to me. In my old-world Italian family, if you put one foot wrong, you were ostracized for many years."

The three shrinks speak in unison. "Ostracized, ja, like circumcised, only not as bad."

Thomas continues: "They would send me a guilt card every three months. I'll bet you didn't know that Hallmark had them available only in Italian and Jewish neighborhoods. Every card always said the same thing, that I was killing my mother. Actually they would alternate between killing my mother and killing my father."

"Oh, ja!" Freud interrupts. "Zee Oedipus Complex. You wanted to kill your father and marry your mother. Zis is very goot."

Thomas continues: "They even selected a woman they wanted me to marry. She was the daughter of a family friend."

"Vat did you do?" Adler asks.

"I married her. I married Cindy Esposito. When I look back on it, I guess I didn't want to disappoint my parents, and Cindy was hot."

"Hot! Hot! Tell us more about hot," Jung pleads.

Thomas refuses to discus his sex life with Cindy. "She may have been hot, but we were not well suited. She never stopped talking, and never said anything of value. She was always primping in front of her mirror, and had my money spent before I made it."

"Vas yours a happy marriage?" Adler asks.

"Oh sure, as long as we were fucking."

Ja! Ja! Ja! Tell us more about fucking!

The session lasts 45 minutes. Thomas keeps his composure, although he doesn't answer many questions. Freida walks with him through the waiting room and opens the door for him to leave.

A few hours later Rose finds Thomas and tells him the results.

"There was a unanimous verdict by the three psychiatrists that you did not care enough about their feelings to share your sexual experiences. They recommended to me that you be put on the observation list. They don't recommend probation because the next step after that is demotion to a lower Sector. You would then be required to go to Sector D, which is reserved for people who have done more Harm than Good. I am very upset about this. It is my responsibility to see that you are assimilated properly and completely into Sector C. Won't you try harder to think of others?"

Thomas drifts through space for quite a while. When he sees Rose he asks her many questions.

"Rose, you say that our mental images are combining. We both know what a flower looks like, and how a saxophone sounds, so we can communicate. What about people who were blind or deaf from birth? What about Helen Keller, who couldn't see or hear? How are their dreams manifested in the AfterWorld? What about infants who perished? They weren't old enough to really have a consciousness of life. What about cats, dogs, and monkeys, who must have some thought capacity? I feel very sorry for all these poor people... er... and animals."

"Speaking of animals, Thomas, I smell a rat. I have the distinct impression that you're telling me what I want to hear. Just remember one thing, you can't fool Room 214. What we all want to see are actions. They speak louder than thoughts."

★

"Rose, can I have my own Room? I'd like to start a Communications Room. I don't care how it's designated."

"You can have one eventually, but not until you have reached Step 5, Enlightenment, or by special decree from Room 214."

Thomas protests. "It will take too long for me to reach Enlightenment and the communications are happening right now. It's important to the Sector for me to analyze them."

"You do have a point about the usefulness of your information. I have an idea. You can sublet part of a Room. It will still be known as whatever room it is, but there will be a subtitle on the Room door that identifies what you are doing. It's very difficult to get Beings to share space with an entity of a different persuasion because it can confuse those who are visiting."

Thomas searches for a very long time but doesn't have any luck finding a space. Rose puts the word out to others in the Sector that Thomas is looking.

"Hey man, what's happening?"

"Hello, Janis! I do love that burgundy red Mercedes convertible."

"Hop in, I found you a cool pad. It's just a few blinks down from Room 27. It's in Room PAP."

"What is Room PAP?"

"Puerile American People, reality TV shows. They will be happy to sublet you a space in the back. There is a connection, right? Media types come in there. Ain't that communications?"

"Very neat, thank you, Janis."

"You're welcome, man. I'll drop you off here, right in front. Go on in and introduce yourself. Bye, hon."

"Hi there, I'm Thomas, and Janis told me you have a sublet space for me out back."

"Hello Thomas, my name is Jennifer Lyon, pleased to meet you. This is a very freaky Room. We've only been in existence a short while. As you know, reality TV shows are a recent phenomenon, and most of the people involved are still alive. We may not have quantity, but we do have quality. There's Ryan Jenkins, Frankie Abernathy, Phil Harris, Joseph Cemiglia, Pedro Zamora, Julien Hug, Nathan Clutter, Kandice Hutchinson, Margaretta Froark, and about two dozen people who worked on the sets, in production, and that sort of thing. Of course, we're all dead or we wouldn't be here, but you already know that." Jennifer giggles.

"We heard about your fantastic success in analyzing Earth communications, and we were hoping you could eventually get us a live feed into our old shows. Some of them may have been cancelled, and that's what we want to find out. Do you know if Donald Trump's *Apprentice* is still on the air?"

"As of four months ago, when I entered the AfterWorld, it was still going strong. Trump gave up his run for the presidency because he was still under contract for the show. Personally, I think...."

Thomas stops himself from giving an opinion on Donald Trump. He remembers that he's a guest in Room PAP, and he lightens up.

"Jennifer, I will guarantee that some kind of contact will be made. All of us are super-receivers. We just have to learn how to access the information in a formal way. Right now we get only random bits from cellphones, television, computers, and other devices. I'm going to try to pinpoint exactly where these TV signals are coming from, and when the shows will be aired."

Jennifer shows him to his space. It's a large area, about twenty-five by seventy feet, and has five electrical benches completely set up and loaded with testing equipment. He remembers all of this from his labs at MIT, and from his father's amateur radio station in Vermont. He gets to work and concentrates on the task at hand.

Okay, I must find out where these signals are originating and predict when they occur so we can record them. Cellphones are on different frequencies in America, Africa, Europe, and Asia. Television frequencies are a problem because most of the energy bounces off the Ionosphere. I have set up monitoring devices on all available frequencies to see if any signals pass through. Common sense tells me that a very small percentage of the original signal will not bounce but will pass through into Space.

Let's see, cellphone frequencies are between 800 and 1,900 MHZ. In some areas of the world, the frequencies go as low as 450 MHZ. Cellphones put out about 3 watts in cars, and the average power for a hand-held phone is between .075 and 1 watt of power. These waves are picked up by a repeater in a tower and re-transmitted all around the world. I see clear indications that the energy is around us. That conversation in New Jersey between the woman and the guy who knocked up her daughter is a good example of a random reception.

So, on to television. Low-powered stations put out about 1.5 kilowatts, and strong stations about 12 kilowatts. The frequencies are predictable and easy to chart. I must find a guide to all the stations, their frequencies and hours of operation.

After some careful tuning, Thomas is able to isolate the cable preview board that is updated hourly on the screen. He can now select any station that is broadcasting. He develops his own repeater that takes the weak signal and amplifies it so it can be shared by the minds of all in Room PAP.

Everyone in the room successfully receives reality TV shows. He laughs to himself when he watches them. *Real*

Housewives, Jersey Shore, Survivor, The Apprentice: They are beyond hilarious to him but to the others they brings tears. He learns the names of the stars: Snooki, the Kardashians, and Pauly D. The Beings in Room PAP are overjoyed to watch their old shows. They decide they are going to produce their own reality TV show and ask Thomas if he wants to be one of the stars. He declines.

Thomas wanders about the Sector with his new receiver and headphones, listening for stray conversations and interesting radio and television stations. He is so focused on finding cellphone energy that he doesn't see the Being who glides over to him.

"What are you listening to, if I may ask?"

"Oh, hi there, I've got the scanner searching for cellphone conversations as part of a study of modern communications."

"Is your study enigmatic, symbolic, or is there a substantive goal in mind? Do you find that random static electrical charges tend to obscure the rest of the sound spectrum? When you become immersed in non-spiritual stimulation, does it interfere with your own Delta waves?"

"So far I seem to be able to separate out here and there. What is your name, sir?"

"Bill Buckley, pleased to meet you."

"*The* Bill Buckley?"

"There are thousands of us, but I suspect you recollect my unique contributions."

"And how! My father really liked your show, *Firing Line*, and I used to watch it with him when I was in high school. We used to argue all the time. I told him I mostly disagreed with you, but I always had a sneaky admiration for your velvet-smooth Conservatism."

"Please don't use the words 'velvet smooth.' It denotes and connotes Fascism. I heard that you are a fiction author. I wrote several novels myself, you know, and they weren't too bad."

"I know, Mr. Buckley, I remember *The Red Hunter* very well. I really enjoyed it except for the awkward sex scenes."

"What do you want from me? I'm an Irish Catholic."

"What part of Sector C are you from, Mr. Buckley?"

"I'm not, I'm in Sector B, and I know Rose very well."

"Sector B!" Thomas is surprised.

"Is that so strange to you? Judge not, lest ye be judged. You Liberals don't have a monopoly on good deeds. I'm on my way to visit a friend in Sector D. Do you want to tag along? That is, if you are not too busy charting cellphone signals."

Thomas has never been to Sector D, and he is anxious to go. "Sure, thanks for the invitation. Do you often go there?

"All the time. Some of my best friends are in D. They are just like you except that instead of 60% Good and 40% Bad, they're 60% Bad and 40% Good." Thomas and Bill glide past the Library (Room L) and several blinks later arrive in Sector D.

"Hey Joe, I'd like you to meet a friend of mine. Joe, this is Thomas."

"Pleased to meet you, Thomas. What are that radio and headphones for? Are you a Commie spy?"

"No sir, just monitoring modern cellphone communications at the request of the Committee."

"Who's on this Committee? Have they been checked out, and did they take a loyalty oath? Even up here we can't be too careful."

"I believe the request originated from someone in Room 214."

"Wouldn't you know it, wouldn't you know it. They've infiltrated top levels of our Administration. I'll wager a bottle of your best Jameson Reserve, Buckley, that all of this originated in Room 213. They want to take us over."

Thomas asks Joe a very pointed question. "Joe, have you ever been to Room HS?"

"Room HS, isn't that Room Head Shrink, full of those psychiatrists? Of course not. They come and visit me here all the time. I've got the first five years of *Playboy* magazine in my room. They fill out a report and pretend they are counseling me, but in reality they just sit in a corner and drool over the Playmates. So I guess a Liberal is just a Conservative who's lying to himself. As the late great Jackie Gleason once said, 'Har har hardy har har.'"

"Pleased to meet you, Joe. If I hear any clandestine Pinko activity, I'll let you know."

★

Rose explains to Thomas what he must do to pass the second series of tests to get his Explorer status. He has asked her many times about the SlingShot after hearing about planet DeJive from Janis. When you become an Explorer, you can travel to other Sectors unaccompanied, and visit other Worlds. After hearing Joe blame Room 213 for all his Sector's imaginary troubles, Thomas is curious to learn more about it.

He leaves Rose and glides for a long while. He figures out how to cloak himself so he isn't detected. He appears as an electrical anomaly, and sneaks past some scary Beings into the NetherWorld. He arrives at a smoldering, gaseous sphere with the sounds of sharp clanging, gunfire, screaming, and moaning. The circle's appearance quickly changes. It is suddenly painted orange with a black circle around it, and a diagonal black line down the center.

"Thomas, damn it! I said you can't visit other Sectors or Room 213 unless you are accompanied by someone in Sector B or higher! The NetherWorld is strictly forbidden for anyone who isn't Enlightened. Why don't you listen? Everything you do is being watched by Room 214. When you do a few more things to piss them off, you'll be right back in Room HS. I wouldn't rely on *their* judgment, if I were you."

"I'm sorry, I was just curious. That's some scary shit. Is that why it's painted orange with a black circle around it?"

"You painted it with your mind, but that's very good, and I'm going to use the image to help others. That's the universal 'stop' or 'no' sign. That's good progress. Listen Thomas, you never stop growing and learning here. As a matter of fact, your actual life on Earth was just the beginning. The religions of the world have it all wrong. You don't sit happily like a vegetable gawking at all the pretty angels. Your actual life was a blip in the continuum. It was like the seed of a redwood tree. The growth of the actual tree happens here. It's up to you whether you want to become a beautiful tall specimen, or a dickweed. You got, that Higher Life Form?"

Thomas has not seen that side of Rose before. She is truly angry with him, but instead of his being upset, it just turns him on.

"Rose, would you like to go for a Swirl?"

"You use that word one more time, Higher Life Form, and I will personally request that you be put in a Containment Room and left there until the next millennium. Is that clear? I'd have better luck trying to herd cats."

"Ha ha, I've *herd* that one before, Rose. I just like you very much. My mind says you are smiling. Are you smiling?"

Rose grabs Thomas but doesn't tell him where they are going.

4

Rose, because she has reached an advanced stage of Enlightenment way beyond others in Sector B, has powers of motion that few have. As she drags him along, Thomas can't resist her great strength. Thomas thinks that Rose carrying him is like a Green Bay Packers linebacker carrying a small chicken. (He still has trouble with bad metaphors.) They are moving so fast that everything is a blur. He hears some sounds and sees some streaking lights, but then all is black. She decelerates and comes to a complete stop.

They are in the middle of Deep Space. He hears and sees nothing. It's somewhat like Room Total Peace, except there is no wonderful Aurora Panorama. Thomas is still holding his receiver and headphones.

"Your next step is to achieve Explorer status. Okay, Higher Life Form, find your way back to Sector C." In a flash, Rose disappears completely, and Thomas is left alone.

"Wait, come back, that's not very loving, you sanctimonious hussy! Why did you to this to me? Where am I?"

Thomas puts on his headphones and tunes his receiver to 800 MHZ, the American cellphone band. He is surprised to hear conversations, but they are several years old. Then he remembers that radio waves travel at the speed of light, 186,000 miles a second, or 700 million miles an hour. He does the math. 700 million MPH times three years = Holy Spumoni!

He glides as fast as he can in one direction, but the cellphone conversations are getting fainter. He hears horrible chatter coming from the NetherWorld. He reverses his direction and glides at hyper-speed. The conversations are back to the way they were. He continues in this direction, and every day or so, he listens on the headphones. The conversations are louder still and are now only seven months old. He continues moving toward the cellphone radio waves, and an Earth week later he is back in the Milky Way Galaxy. He's proud of himself for navigating back into the Sector. He was traveling at an astronomical rate of speed.

He sees Earth and wonders if he can monitor conversations. He glides to a place in the upper atmosphere above New England in the U.S.A. He listens to a complete jumble of chatter. He uses the special bandpass filter he developed back in Room PAP to isolate the conversations. He is able to fine-tune northern New England, and finally Burlington, Vermont. He is also able to hear WPBS, which broadcasts from the top of Mount Mansfield. He hears a show about to begin on the hour. He was about to turn it off when the announcer said something of interest.

"Greetings, this is *In Your Backyard,* and I'm your host, Kathy Howell. It's been six months since the untimely death of Thomas Buchetta. His third novel, *The Princess and the Pauper*, has been number one on the New York Times best-seller list for two straight months. It is also number one on Kindle and tops the e-book list. With us today is his former wife, Cindy Buchetta, and her new husband, Ronald Wright.

"Cindy, what was Thomas Buchetta's inspiration for this great book? It's a finalist for the National Book Award, and there's talk it may also be mentioned for a Pulitzer."

"He was always very quiet and secretive, but I know I was the inspiration for the Princess. He probably used himself for the Pauper."

"How many copies has it sold so far, if you don't mind my asking?"

"It's difficult to say, because we don't have final totals for the last two months. His agent, well, he used to be Tom's agent, but now he's my agent, says that it will sell about twenty million copies by the end of the year, plus foreign royalties and movie rights. We get about $2.50 per book."

Thomas is beside himself. "Married! Married! A new husband! That asshole! Fifty million dollars! You sit there smiling and call me a pauper, you ugly piece of garbage!"

"Hello, Thomas, you found your way back very easily. What would you have done if you didn't have your receiver with you?" Rose can see that Thomas is fuming.

"I would have traveled as far away from this Sector as possible."

"I'm sorry you're disappointed, but Cindy has to get on with her life. You shouldn't begrudge her a new husband and new-found wealth."

"Bullshit! I was working in Home Depot and took another shift loading trucks at WalMart to pay the bills. Her new asshole husband was our next-door neighbor. He must have divorced his wife as soon as he found out Cindy was rich. Rich with the money *I* earned. Don't tell me not to begrudge. I'd like to kill the both of them."

"I was afraid it was a mistake to let you translate Earth messages. It's interfering with your path to Enlightenment."

Thomas eventually calms down and realizes that the stimulation and events in the Sector Rooms are much more important and meaningful than his grudge. He continues monitoring tweets and compiling data for the Communications Committee. Rose insists that he stay away from the space above northern New England, U.S.A.

★

"Whoa! Thomas Buchetta, paisano, saluti. I thought most of us came out of Jersey or Brooklyn. How'd you end up in Vermont?"

Thomas notices a thin man with a hairpiece and an infectious smile. "My father moved us from Brooklyn when I was five years old."

"Your old man done good, made a new life for his family. Believe me, it isn't easy coming from nothing to rise to the top. I know, I did it my way. Listen, Thomas, I picked up some energy when I was hanging around Room 27. The gang said you're unhappy in your personal relationships with beings of the female persuasion."

"Who are you?"

"My name is Sinatra, and I'm going to help you get laid. Thomas, Thomas, this isn't college, you have to be more subtle. I'm like you, I make my home in the C Sector. Don't chase after Guides or Beings in the B or A Sectors. They're too hard to get. What you need is a nice D Sector girl. They're the ones who really put out. Don't forget, they are more bad than good. In this case bad translates into loose, like available. You got your Certification, didn't you? How come Rose doesn't let you attend a Swirl?"

"She hates me. She blocks me every time I try."

"Naw, she's just playing hard to get. All those B Sector Guides are the same. They *always* come around sooner or later. You just have to be patient. In the meantime, why don't I introduce you to some really bad women in Sector D. We can pick them up, take them to Room 27, and have a party. I'll sing, you play the sax. Thomas, I'm telling you, it's a sure thing."

"Can we do that now?" Thomas is eager and excited.

Although Thomas isn't supposed to go to other sectors unless accompanied by Beings in higher Sectors, he goes anyway. Frank and Thomas glide to Section D and look around. There are many beautiful women who crisscross in front of them. They immediately recognize Frank and know what he's after. Thomas introduces himself to two D broads.

"Hey, Frank, I want you to meet my two new friends."

"Whoa! Who's the mouse with the built?"

"Her name is Wanda, and this is Sheila."

The four of them waste no time traveling to Room 27, but instead of finding a party in progress, everyone is languid and lying around. The smell of pot smoke is in the air and there are acid tabs on top of the guitar amps.

"Who let this rat in here?" Frank asks Jimi Hendrix.

"I don't know, man. He just wandered in."

"Thomas, this guy is from the very bottom of Sector E, bordering on Sector F. I wouldn't be at all surprised if he ends up in Sector F or lower. Thomas Buchetta, meet Dr. Timothy Leary."

"Ease up on me, Frank, you're too intense. You've got to mellow out. Remember, turn on, tune in, drop out."

"Drop dead, Leary! If you weren't already dead I'd be glad to provide you with that service. There are people in this Room who would be alive today if you hadn't LSD'd them."

"Everyone makes a choice, crooner."

"You make me sick, you disgusting old hippie quack! So you toured around the country with Gordon Liddy to make a few bucks. Richard Nixon was right, you were the most dangerous man in America."

Thomas pushes Timothy Leary over a Fender Super Reverb amp, and the girls scream.

"We're going back home. You two are no fun. Yeah, a real party-pooper you are," Wanda says to Thomas as she walks out."

Thomas is in big trouble. No matter what disagreements you have with other Beings, you do not initiate violence. Rose brings him into a Containment Room and discusses his behavior.

"Frank did the right thing to call out Leary. I know you were upset, and were protective of those in Room 27. Your violence was not negative violence, but positive violence. Naturally this is all symbolic, but you wreaked absolute havoc with Leary's ego. However, do not do this again, because every act of violence, every violent thought, registers in Room 214. Yours are piling up, after that cellphone incident with your wife. Time to cool it."

★

Thomas makes several trips to Room TP in between listening to and cataloguing random tweets. He pays an occasional visit to Room 27. The disgraced Dr. Leary hasn't been back there, and the group is much more lively. Rose helped Thomas prep for the second series of Explorer tests (the first being finding his way back to Sector C). He took the tests and passed easily. He was doing so well, they let him take the third series ahead of time. He passed those also. Thomas has questions for Rose.

"How does a warped brain fit in here? Many people are bipolar without medication, sociopathic because of chemical imbalances, abusers because they were highly traumatized by others. They are as much victims as criminals. Are they categorized as more good than bad, or vice versa? I met someone in Free Space that had to be at least three sandwiches short of a picnic. How can this person pass his/her tests to achieve Explorer status?"

"Thomas, I detect more than a little discomfort in your being around people you don't want to picnic with. This is absolutely normal. Their thoughts may seem to us incoherent, but they sometimes have a defined purpose. They are allowed to wander around at will as long as they don't harm anyone. Those who interfere with life forms in the Sector are taken to Room HR & S after they visit Room HS. You already met the doctors in Room HS. Room HR & S, House of Representatives and Senate, is where they are taken when their behavior is judged by Room HS as being antisocial. It takes many years of treatment before they can abandon their delusional state and rejoin normal Sentient Beings in the Sector."

Thomas does further research into wireless computers, particularly Wi-Fi applications. His briefly-widowed wife worked for a computer programmer who specialized in those networks. He remembers her using the wireless ad-hoc network for computer-to-computer communications. There are over four million hotspots for people to exchange signals, and more than eight hundred million Wi-Fi devices are sold every year.

Cindy's boss was one of the pioneers who developed Wi-Fi Direct in 2010 using a new discovery and security technology. She has built-in security codes for her computer, so it's nearly impossible for him to listen in with his PAP Room receivers. Thomas sets out to discover a way to hack into her computer.

A Wi-Fi signal occupies five channels in the 2.4 GHz band. He knows that channels 1, 6, and 11 comprise the only group of three non-overlapping channels in the United States. Many of these devices have a range of only thirty-five feet. Cindy used a phone modem in her computer, and she could access the Internet using the same repeaters that cellphones use. She took her damned laptop with her even when they went on vacation or to the lake. If only he can figure out the codes, the amplified antenna in his receiver is sensitive enough to hear her signal. He can then transfer it to the thought processor for him to read.

After many sessions of trial and error, he succeeds in isolating Cindy's computer frequency and hacks into her protective codes. He can't send anything or see her stored files, but he can receive the e-mail messages that are sent to her. He spends many hours reading her mail and is totally bored. She is as boring up here as she was down there. Rose is not happy that he is obsessing about his past life on Earth.

"Thomas, you are here, she is there. Here is where you are going to be for a long time, actually for all time. There is no more 'time' here, not in the final measurement. It is Infinity. Do you understand? When we talk of weeks or years, it's only so you can have a basis for comparison. Do not be concerned with your past on Earth. That is but one dot in the continuum. You will be here long after the Earth, its Sun, and this entire Galaxy have disappeared. So what Cindy does is really diddly squat."

Rose knows when Thomas is really listening, and when he is just nodding his head in agreement. She knows full well he is up to something, but he is clever enough not to telegraph it. She resigns herself to react, rather than try to anticipate his every move. Room 214 already knows he is a difficult Initiate, and her Guide status is not in jeopardy.

Thomas refuses to accept the boundaries that have been placed on his movements. He circles the Earth looking for escaping signals, and again wanders over northern New England. He tunes in to Cindy's cellphone frequency while she is in the middle of a conversation with her mother. Thomas hears the TV in the background, the same TV that had been in his bedroom. He also hears the same squeaks he heard just before he slammed into the side of that cement truck. He remembers where they come from.

"Fucking bitch! Those squeaks are our old box springs. You kinky piece of shit! You talk on your cellphone while you rut. You were screwing the asshole next-door neighbor while you were talking to me on the phone. I died because you are a whore. You will pay for this, somehow, some way. I will get you, so help me."

Thomas returns to Room PAP and devises a plan. If he can summon enough energy from the Sector, he can gather it and transmit it back to Earth and into Cindy's computer. He studies all the radiant and stray electrical energy in the Galaxy but finds them too haphazard to gather and control. What he needs is one huge burst of energy that he can capture and send Earthbound. He finally figures out how he can do it. He leaves Room PAP and glides to the center of Sector C. He has his receiver ready to capture the energy, and his special transmitter to send the energy and his message to Cindy's computer.

"GOD! GOD! GOD! GOD! GOD! GOD! GOD! GOD! GOD!"

Thomas shouts over and over. Every Being in the Sector is aroused and alarmed, and they all beam their energy toward him. He collects it, amplifies it, and sends his message Earthbound.

5

Back in Burlington, Vermont, in the U.S.A., Cindy and her husband Ronald are lying in bed. He is watching a Red Sox baseball game on FOX with his headphones on so he doesn't disturb Cindy, who is writing e-mails on her computer. There is a bowl of popcorn between them, and Cindy's Chihuahua, Taco, is at her feet, eating the bits that Cindy absentmindedly tosses his way.

"Oh, crap!"

"What's the matter, dear?" Ronald takes off his headphones to ask.

"I think I've got a computer virus. I can't seem to delete this message. It keeps appearing on my notepad browser."

"Why don't you open it and see what it is?"

"You don't know anything, do you? I can't open it; it could contain a virus that will destroy my data."

Cindy tries to sign off the computer, but Thomas has positioned his message to be uploaded like a Microsoft update that is beyond the control of the user. The file is automatically transferred to her "My Documents" folder. She reads the message when it puts itself on her screen:

"You pig, you absolutely disgusting, whore-pig. You were screwing that asshole while you were talking to me on your cellphone, you perverted little slimeball. I was distracted, and it cost me my life. You are a cheap, narcissistic, manipulative, selfish little slit and a poor excuse for any resemblance of being a woman. You are a dirty cunt, a filthy, lying, bitch, pig, whore, slut, slob, and a rotten piece of garbage. I only married you to keep my parents quiet. You will pay dearly. I will get you! I will get both of you!"

Cindy screams and throws her computer away from her. It hits Taco on the head, killing him instantly.

The entire C and B Sectors are aroused, and Room 214 calls Rose in for a consultation. She confirms that she told Thomas not to use "the word," but he deliberately did so to capture the collective energy and send it back to Earth. This has never been done before, that a confirmed dead person has left actual, tangible evidence of their visit to an alive Human's computer. The Prime Directive has been violated. Thomas's interference with a living Sentient Being was bad enough. His motive made things even worse. Room 214 has recognized that he has special communications skills and has given him much latitude to refine his ability. It was always taken for granted that, since he was studying for assimilation into Sector C, he was more good than bad. After Rose read the message he sent Cindy, it was determined that Thomas sent negative energy for the purpose of doing harm. Because of the seriousness of his actions, it was decided to skip probation and go straight to punishment. Rose glides over to Thomas, who is chortling gleefully while he does cartwheels in Earth's upper Troposphere.

"Does doing evil things make you happy?" Rose asks with sadness in her voice.

"She had it coming for a long time. Evil must be punished."

"Evil must never be punished by doing more and greater evil. Your message.....and what about that message?.....you don't like women very much do you?"

"She's not a woman she's a cu...."

"I don't want to hear it, Thomas. She read your message, threw her Hewlett Packard Notebook computer into the air, and it landed on her pet Chihuahua's skull, crushing it instantly."

Thomas chortles and does another cartwheel.

"What I have here is a statement that was written for you by the staff in Room 214. I'm going to read it now because you need to know what has to come next. They spoke in terms that are not particularly gentle. Since you appreciate directness, perhaps that will help your understanding."

Rose reads the message from Room 214.

"Thomas, in spite of all Rose's cautions and her good example, you have insisted on disregarding the guidelines and rules she has so meticulously put in your path. When there is a final sorting out, you will be judged, not by how brilliant you are, or how clever, but how kind. Kindness and truth are much more important than ambition and competence. You have misled your Guide into thinking that you had no ulterior motives in your Earth communications. We knew that it was just a matter of time before you gave in to your own negative feelings. You used Rose to position yourself to interfere with life forms on Earth, in blatant violation of the Prime Directive. Although you are not basically an Evil Being, there are many elements in your nature that are not good. Actually some of them are not worth a flying fuck.

"It is the will of the staff in Room 214 that you experience the full force of the dark side you are embracing. Your ability to manipulate others and your habit of trying to gain an advantage in every situation is hereby officially terminated. From now on there is going to be a direct A = A reaction between what you do and its effects on yourself and those around you. It is the decision of Room 214 to drastically demote you to another Sector, to be decided by the horrible Beings in the NetherWorld. You have experienced the death of your own conscience. In many ways, your better self has died."

Thomas is no longer manic but pensive and worried. "Rose, does this mean that I have to leave Sector C? What do they mean, my better self has died? I thought I was already dead."

"There are many kinds of death, Thomas. Death of the body is just one of them. There's the death of hope, the death of goodness, the death of kindness, the death of..."

Rose stops talking because she is too upset to continue. Thomas sees that she is crying.

"Thomas, you are to report to Room 213 in the NetherWorld for reassignment."

With that final statement, Rose disappears into Deep Space.

"No! Wait! I'm sorry. I won't do it again." Thomas pleads but is answered with empty silence. He tries to access room TP but is denied. Janis pulls alongside him in her Mercedes.

"You blew it, man, you've got a rough gig ahead of you. You might need this." She hands him his Mark IV Selmer tenor sax, and speeds away.

★

The next day, Cindy composes herself. She has been talking with her mother, a first-class piranha of the eighth magnitude, about her communication with her dead husband. Her mother tells her not to worry. She tells Cindy that she has all the money, a new husband she can easily control, and the ability to turn off the computer any time she wants. She reassures her that Thomas Buchetta cannot do her any damage.

"He probably wrote that before he died and found a way to send it to your computer." She tells her daughter that ghosts and the occult are not real. Cindy changes her e-mail provider to direct dial-up just in case. She senses that Thomas has infiltrated her wireless system.

Cindy says, "The only way he can interfere with my life is to read my mind. He's just a baccala who likes to hear himself talk. Thank you, Thomas, for setting me up for life, you poor bastard, wherever you are."

Thomas tries to access Cindy's cellphone and computer but has no success. The receiver in Room PAP is inoperative. All it gets is static and reality TV shows. Thomas can no longer monitor Tweet, Twitter, Twang, Twat, Twipple, or Twap. All he can get are reruns of 1970s sitcoms. He has been effectively cut off from all modern communications and has been turned out of Room PAP. He has no choice but to glide through the Galaxy to Room 213. He is in no hurry and merely saunters along, studying the Beings who drift parallel or perpendicular to his path. As he enters Sector T, Thomas spies a strange entity.

"Hello, who are you?" he asks nervously.

"I'm a Composite. My name is Mary, Henry, Ralph, George, Fanny, Hermann, Ilsa, Sylvester, times seven to the nth."

Thomas misses Rose's counsel. She would have known what a Composite is. He has entered NetherWorld and is only a few blinks away from Room 213.

"I can see by your blank expression that you have never encountered a Composite before. I am 50,000 Beings rolled into one. I have the power of an Earth city, and none of us cares how much harm we do. I am a wonderful collection of SS storm troopers, Torquemada's torturers, Republican economists, environmental rapists, and fundamentalist religious fanatics who persecute anyone who is not just like themselves. I move very slowly through Sector T, lumbering along. Nobody fucks with me, especially not those wimps in Sector B. They are very fast and can slip around me, but one on one against me, they are dogmeat. We don't leave the NetherWorld, and seldom leave Sector T, but occasionally patrol the extremity to ensure that the 214 group in the EtherWorld doesn't increase their domain. I can see that you are a defrocked C Sector Being who is on his way to Room 213. If you were just visiting, I would have swallowed your insides for lunch. Keep on going. 213 is on your left."

Thomas enters Room 213 and is greeted by a generic sadist who smiles as he sticks a long pin into Thomas's arm, drawing blood.

"What was that for?"

"It's standard procedure here. We send the sample to our chef. You never know, you could wind up as our dessert tonight."

Thomas enters a room that is rather lively. There's a harem displaying every sexual position imaginable, while they entertain brigands who are partying and shouting. They are all drinking American bourbon and chasing it down with dove blood. A huge Being approaches Thomas and welcomes him to Room 213.

"I'm Attila the Hun, but my friends just call me Hun, and I think it's sweet. So, you might be one of us. This is very good. We don't believe in understanding, vegetarianism, or in a peaceful resolution to anything. Let me tell you about my life. We crossed the Rhine into Roman Gaul. I had such a good time fighting the Gauls. It brings tears to my eyes just thinking about it. But first, let me introduce you to some of our clan. You probably know Adolph, Josef, and Mao, Benito, and the rest of the boys. I was listening to Earth communications on my Nether equipment and I heard this song about a neat place. Did you ever eat at Alice's Restaurant? They talked about mother rapin' and father stabbin'. Now that's my kind of gourmet."

"No, I never ate there," Thomas replies, "but I did eat at a Ray's Pizzeria in Manhattan in the same spot where a mob hit splattered two guys all over the table."

"Excellent! Let me tell you what I did when I attacked the Gauls. I cut the lead man's head off. Naturally blood spurted all over the place. His head fell off and rolled down the hill going kerplonk, kerplonk, toward the other Gauls. As it skipped over the rocks, the others freaked out and ran down the hill. Well, it was a beautiful sight to behold. We had the high ground and charged down the hill after them cutting off all their heads. All you could hear was kerplonk, kerplonk, kerplonk, and all you could see was heads rolling down the hill like a bunch of tennis balls spilled out of a canvas bag. (Attila also has trouble with bad metaphors.) It was the high point of my life.

"Let me introduce you to The Chopper. Hey Chopper, meet Thomas."

On Earth, Chopper was never caught for his crimes. He terrorized the part of Eastern Europe known as Transylvania, in the sixteenth century. He would dismember anyone who was too tall, too short, too fat, or too thin. He has only four teeth in his mouth. They are all in front, sharpened to a point, and covered with titanium.

Chopper speaks. "Thomas, we're proud of you for scaring the shit out of your wife Cindy. We have some other ideas that you will love to hear. Did you ever see the movie *Psycho*? That Alfred Hitchcock was a real prince. I love the sound of that knife plunging into that bimbo in the shower. I recorded it, and it is the white noise that lulls me to sleep every night. There's nothing quite like the gushing and mushing of tushes when they are sliced up with a good broadax, or any sharp blade. I find it much more satisfying than a gun. It's more immediate and personal, sweet music, don't you think?"

Thomas is given a hearty meal of roast lamb, young stuffed quail, ground-up chipmunk, poached kitten livers, and steamed gerbil brains. The bourbon served with every course has a red tint. He is afraid to ask why. He is seated at a long table with thirty people on either side. There is no chair at the right end, but there is at the far end on the left side. A Being sits down and everyone says "All Hail!" in unison. Thomas doesn't know what to do, so he also stands up and says "All Hail!" but is a full beat behind the others. They all glare at him, but because he is new, they do nothing. Chopper, who is sitting next to Thomas, identifies the Being as Beelzie the Bub, the high roller. Beelzie the Bub welcomes him to their gathering and asks everyone at the table to give Thomas a round of applause.

"That was a magnificent display of ingenuity to send that message to your ratbag ex-wife. We picked up her reaction on our Nether receiver. How did you summon the energy to hack into her computer?"

Thomas says, "I used the secret word, a duck dropped down, and every Being in the Sector put out all the energy I needed. I then redirected it toward my dear Cindy's computer. You should have heard her scream. Killed that fucking dog. He used to hump the ankle of every guest we had in the house. I used to kick him when Cindy wasn't looking. When that computer cracked his skull, it made me very happy."

Everyone at the table pounds their tankards on the dark wood. They all begin chanting, "Cracked skulls are happiness, cracked skulls are happiness. More like that, more like that."

★

Beelzie the Bub decides to enroll Thomas in Treachery Training. There are Rooms in Sector T like there are in Sector C. Thomas has nothing better to do, and since he can't go back to his former home, he really doesn't have much choice. There are too many pitfalls to wandering alone in the Universe. He remembers Rose telling him that, in certain areas, an unaccompanied Being could be assimilated quickly by giant amoeba-like Entities. He wouldn't have enough time to try to summon Room TP. Now that option has been removed, and Thomas thinks it best not to go it alone.

Room TTC, the Treachery Training Center, has a strangely familiar look about it. There's a blue carpet with gold designs, and one hundred desks are arranged in a semicircle around a center podium with flags on either side. There's a balcony with seats. Behind the seats are gold wallpaper and many doors. There are seats on either side of the podium, which has a microphone upon it. The 100 chairs are straight-back seats with arms and look very old. The Vice Trainer welcomes Thomas, who is sitting in the last row on the right. Refreshments are brought out to the 100 trainees. Thomas sees a bowl of soup and red bourbon. He asks the person next to him what is in the soup.

"They caught him entering the Sector yesterday. He's being recycled."

Thomas jumps up from his chair and vomits all over the blue carpet. Two heavyweights escort him out of the Chamber....er....Training Center. He is taken to a small area about the size of an American medical examining room. After five minutes he is greeted by a man with a long scar running from above his left eye to below the bottom of his chin.

"Looks like you're not quite ready for Treachery Training, see? You're going to have to ease into it, see? We're sending you to an inactive part of the Sector that we reserve for pansies, see? You will be home tutored in the fine arts until you are ready to resume advanced training, see?"

The heavy gives Thomas back his Mark IV Selmer saxophone, which has been plugged up with dried manure mixed with concrete. He leaves it in the Room and goes to his new home, which is in Sector T, Room CS, the Chicken Shit Room.

Beelzie the Bub gathers Hun, Adolph, Josef, and ten of his closest advisors and formulates a plan based on what Thomas has told them.

"Okay, listen up, here's what we're going to do. If that wimp Thomas can hack into a computer, so can we. We have to decide where we can do the most damage, perhaps some military security system, or nuclear plant protection circuit."

Hun says, "He may be a wimp, but he knows his shit. We may need him to crack the codes."

Beelzie says, "He doesn't have the stomach for it, but I know what we can do. We'll tell him we want to....let me see here.... I've got it. We'll tell him we want to contact our loved ones left behind. We may be bad, but we still miss them."

"Mine have been dead for sixteen hundred years, and I killed most of them myself," Hun says as he swigs some red bourbon.

Beelzie continues, "I'll bet I know how he did it. He used the D·O·G word. Once we have chosen our target, we will use the, ooops, I almost said it. I'll spell it backwards. The P·O·G word to summon all the energy in Sector T. Looks like we will be having some fun, boys."

6

*H*un was chosen to be Thomas's Guide and Personal Trainer. Beelzie desperately wants the codes to some coordinates where he can concentrate Sector T energy to do the most damage. He knows that Thomas can provide them. He knows another enticement that hardly ever fails.

Hun glides to Room CS. "Hello, Thomas, I'd like you to meet Diphtheria. Diphtheria, this is Thomas."

Diphtheria is a large woman and is the only person that Thomas has seen so far in Sector T who has all his or her teeth. She is extremely aggressive and tells Hun to leave them alone for a while. She takes out a photo album showing 11,376 different ways to have sex, and asks Thomas to pick one. She proudly tells him that she has personally tested all the positions and possibilities, and can vouch for their effectiveness. He sees her put on some perfume from a small glass bottle. It smells like rotting cabbage.

"Listen, dahling, I rejected over 20,000 before coming up with these 11,376."

Thomas doesn't know what to do. He is completely turned off by Diphtheria but is afraid if he says no, she will ruin his private parts for his entire AfterWorld. He desperately tries to think of a way out.

"Diphtheria, I'm so glad you're here. I could use some help setting up this equipment. There's a sex show coming from Earth that has a bunch of new positions that you could put in your book."

She jumps at the chance, and Thomas is relieved when he succeeds in accessing the porn channel from someplace in America on the NetherReceiver. She snaps photos from the monitor with her camera. Hun returns to take her back to the harem. Diphtheria kisses Thomas (ick) and thanks him for the neat new stuff. Hun is extremely impressed that he could access pornography. "Beelzie will think more kindly of you."

Thomas wants out. He decides that wandering alone in the Universe is preferable to staying in Room Chicken Shit. He gathers a NetherReceiver and headphones and glides several blinks from his room.

"Going somewhere?" A Composite is following him.

"No, sir." He thinks quickly. "I'm just headed to the edge of Sector T to pick up and analyze some stray communications."

"We'll accompany you." Thomas sees three Composite Beings, who quickly surround him. They can easily match his speed, so they must be much faster than he. He knows he can't outrun them. He listens to his receiver for a while and watches violent X-rated movies on the monitor. It seems that all family shows are filtered out in the T Sector. All that's available are movies about gladiator fights, people dying in drug wars, films about natural disasters like earthquakes and floods, and the transcripts from the 102nd Congress. He can see some faint stars at the edge of the EtherWorld, and it makes him homesick. He decides not to make a run for it and goes back to Room CS.

★

Rose is summoned to Room 214. She is now part of the Room staff and has been promoted to Sector A. The staff throws her a party, and she is given a bottle of her favorite wine, a 1929 Bordeaux. There is a long table with thirty chairs on either side. There is no chair on the left end, but there is one on the right end. The guests are jovial and having a good time. They are eating rum cake, chocolate mousse, and cannoli, wonderful memories for all the staff.

Suddenly, a Supreme Being enters the Room. He/She sits in the chair at the right head of the table. All the staff sees are lights, more beautiful than the Aurora Borealis. The actual Being is hidden among them. Her/His fame is legendary on Earth, and people call the Being by many different names: Allah, The Father, Jehovah, Yahwah, Immanuel, Lord, Ishvar, Rama, Wakan Tanka, Money (in America), and many others. For purposes of clarity, and because most of the names on Earth refer to male deities, the Supreme Being will be referred to as "He" from now on.

He has never spoken His name, and the people on His staff don't think He has one. It is up to the believer to give Him a name, and naturally they are all different. Unfortunately, Humans kill each other over these names, but don't realize that they are all talking about the same Supreme Being. About 400 years ago, His staff voted on a name for the Supreme Being and came up with *Jake*. His lights are not shining as brightly as usual, and His staff senses that something is the matter. Jake speaks:

"We have a problem that I didn't foresee. Yeah, yeah, I'm supposed to know everything. For Christ's sake, even I need a break once in a while. When we sent Thomas away to study evil so he can make a final choice, I forgot about his ability to harness energy and redirect it toward Earth. I don't think he will tell anyone in the NetherWorld how he did it, but Beelzie is very clever and will probably figure it out. He will then turn to Thomas for code breaking and other technical support to do his evil deeds. So, there has been a change in plans. Here's what I want you to do."

★

Thomas wanders outside his Room, again with his NetherReceiver. The Composite Beings track him as usual. This time he moves very slowly, stopping to listen to his headphones. He is so sad and remorseful, he decides that if his fate is to be consumed by these horrible creatures, it is better than living among them. He puts on a burst of speed and catapults ahead of the three Composites. He catches them off guard, and it takes them awhile to make out his direction. He is headed out of Sector T. They are very clumsy, but they make up lost ground and are but a few blinks behind him.

"Hop in, man! Get rid of that piece of junk NetherReceiver. It's too heavy and will slow us down."

Janis is driving, only without her middle-aged disguise. In the back seat is Rose. One of the Composites sends an evil-energy burst from 50,000 murderers toward the Mercedes, while the other Composites seal the escape route out of Sector T. Janis evades the energy burst with a quick right turn. One of the Composites shouts "GOP!, GOP!, GOP!," and instantly every being in T is aroused. Janis drives her car at hyper-speed, weaving in and out, avoiding Composites, which are everywhere. She crosses a double yellow line and doesn't stop at the NetherTrain crossing. Everyone in the T Sector thinks she is headed out toward Sector C in the EtherWorld, but she fools them by making a U turn and driving right into the heart of Sector T, toward Room 213. She buzzes Beelzie, who is standing outside. He is beside himself with rage. Janis exits Sector T from the other side toward Deep Space. There she has all the advantage because she is ten times faster than the Composites. She does a 270-degree hyper-loop and enters her World through the back door.

Janis drops Rose off at Room 214, but not before Thomas tries to give Rose a kiss.

"No sex between Initiates and Guides, remember?"

"But I'm not an Initiate, I'm an Explorer."

"You never stop, do you? If you so much as say the wrong word to the wrong person, you will wind up back in the NetherWorld. The only reason you're here is because the knowledge you possess poses a great threat to mankind if Beelzie gets his hands on it. If I ever catch you telling the truth about something, I might invite you for tea." Rose disappears.

"Don't look at *me* that way. You are becoming a real drag," Janis says to Thomas. "I'm a one-Room woman, and it's Room 27."

Janis drives Thomas to Sector D and leaves him off in Room MR, the Muckraker Room. It's the same room that Joe McCarthy is in.

"Okay hon, here's...."

"Janis, please don't call me 'hon.' There's an evil being in the Netherworld, Beelzie's inner circle, and his name is also Hun, spelled with a U instead of an O."

"That's okay, hon, just as long as you remember how to spell. It will do you good to remember those cuties, keeps you from misbehaving. You aren't subletting space here like you did in Room PAP in Sector C, but you do have a nice Room full of all that groovy shit you like to play with. See if you can stay out of trouble."

Thomas says hello to Joe and settles into his new space. The rest of the people in the Room, which is huge, are mostly politicians and some others who caused trouble on Earth. There's George Wallace and his States Rights group, Vladimir Lenin and a group of Bolsheviks, Pancho Villa, Warren G. Harding (too many scandals during his administration), plus several coveys of notables.

Thomas sees Joe again in the sitting area. "It must really chap you to have to share a Room with Lenin."

"We don't speak."

"This is a rather lively group. What do Pancho Villa and Warren G. Harding have in common?"

"You don't really have to ask that, if you stop and think about it."

Thomas is grateful to be back in the EtherWorld, but very battered. He remembers Room TP and immediately goes there. He is again comforted by the Aurora Panorama and the quiet sounds of music and nature. He remembers the time he squirted his neighbor's cat with his garden hose and badly frightened it. The cat was coming toward him to be petted, and he betrayed the cat's trust. He thinks about the computer message he sent to Cindy, and Rose's observation that he must have a really low opinion of women. Instead of being at peace, he remembers those things he'd done that were evil.

Rose is suddenly next to him in the Room, and Thomas does a triple-diagonal turn before he resumes his position.

"Sorry to startle you, but as you know, your Guide can also come in here."

Thomas gives Rose a hug. She was about to slam him, but she realized it wasn't a sexual hug.

"I'm glad to see you. Are you still my Guide?"

"Yes, I am. You are the last Initiate I am to Guide. Since I've been promoted to Sector A, and made part of Room 214 staff, I have other duties. Purchasing, inventory, accounting, backorders, things like that."

"What!" Thomas is surprised.

"Sure, I'm low person on the totem pole. Somebody's got to do those things, although I admit that I miss the field work. That's why I'm here. I can see you're unhappy, even though you are in Room Total Peace. The reason for that is uncleansed badness that is still part of your memory. We all have those thoughts, and they stay with us forever. If we have too many of them because we have led evil lives, our AfterWorld is tormented. That's what humans mean when they use the world Hell."

Thomas is sweating. "You mean I was in Hell? I thought that was in the NetherWorld."

"They are the same, and you may be there again, if Room 214 decides your deeds are rotten enough to warrant permanent reassignment. The good news, that most humans don't realize, is that you can undo some of the evil by recognizing and acknowledging it. Religious people call it *atonement*. You have recognized it. Now it's up to you to take the next step."

★

Outside Sector D, just one blink away from Thomas's new Room MR, there's a bar called Gabriel's Hideaway. It is *the* most popular day spot in this part of the EtherWorld. It's not called a nightspot, because most of the time it's dark up here. Concentrated light is a rare occurrence (notice how tiny those little stars are), so the Beings hang out where there are fabulous lights. There are four bars that form a square, each exactly 1250 feet long. In the center of Gabriel's are tables and a nice fountain. Beings have thrown coins and other objects in it for good luck.

Joe and Thomas are about to sit down on two stools in the West bar, but Thomas is intrigued by the large fountain. It doesn't contain water, but a light show similar to the grand finale of a fireworks display. He sees the objects that have been thrown in for good luck. There's a Roman coin with Constantine on the face. A Byzantine coin with Leo the Wise on it. A bunch of drachmas, an ancient Icelandic fertility symbol, and a small carved goddess figure that looks very old. There are medals from the Crimean War, a rabbit's foot (symbolic of course), and a 1997 American income tax form that has been savagely ripped apart.

Beings from the entire EtherWorld meet there, including Room 214 Staff. There is security at each of the four entrances. Several clocks ago, a Composite Being drifted undetected across from Sector F and tried to create panic and mayhem. He was stopped by a quick-thinking bartender who doused him with a full pint of warm Guinness stout. That caused the Composite to explode, and some of the Beings didn't make it out the door. They're mounted over the bar on silver plaques. Gabriel's can be a rough place, especially for newcomers.

Joe and Thomas spot Bill Buckley sitting a table near the fountain. They grab their drinks and sit down at the table, which has four seats.

"Why don't you sit at the bar like everyone else, Buckley? You're such an elitist," Joe slurs, almost losing his balance. Bill flashes that sardonic smile, and his tongue briefly flicks from his lips, like a lizard's. Vladimir Lenin and five of his Bolsheviks sit at a table near the East bar. General George Patton joins Bill and his group.

"Who let the Russkies in here?" George asks Bill.

"We should try rapprochement as long as it's with honor. After all, we have to drink in the same bar," Buckley responds.

"Rapprochement, my ass! We're going to have to fight them sooner or later." George raises his raspy voice.

Thomas senses that there's going to be trouble. The Arbitrators are standing by in the event a fight breaks out. In the EtherWorld they don't have bouncers in bars. In the NetherWorld they do. Usually their bouncers produce a sound that goes kerplonk, kerplonk. It's not good to be thrown out of a bar in Sector T, because the top part of your anatomy is usually left behind and gets mounted on a matted yak-fur plaque.

Patton throws a peanut, and it bounces on Lenin's table. One of the Bolsheviks throws two peanuts that bounce on Bill's table. Patton throws half a bag of peanuts at Lenin, and they reciprocate by throwing half a bag at Bill's table. Immediately two Arbitrators intervene and stand between them. One says to the other, "This is how it always starts. First the peanuts, then the ashtrays, then the chairs, then the tables." Patton is asked to leave the bar, since he started the trouble.

★

Thomas is summoned to Room 214, where he meets with members of the EtherWorld Security Committee.

"Thomas, did you willingly or unwillingly give any information, such as codes or our D·O·G name, to Beelzie?"

Thomas puts both hands over his face, wanting to hide. "No, I didn't, but I did brag about hacking into Cindy's computer and killing her dog. In my opinion, it's just a matter of time before they can do the same thing. There are so many sadistic military Beings in T, and they have expertise in destructive hacking."

"Thomas, does Beelzie know how to use energy bursts?"

"He definitely does. When I was rescued by Janis and Rose, I heard one of the Composites yell the P·O·G word. That alerted the entire Sector, in the same way that our D·O·G word does."

"Oh, F·U·C·K!" the Perimeter Defense Chief exclaims. "If they figure out how to get the codes, they will cause great harm on Earth, and many other worlds. Thomas, I'm assigning two senior staff members from Room 214 to accompany you back to Room MR. The three of you will not rest until you create a way to counter the possible use of a Beelzie energy weapon. That is your assignment."

Back in Room MR, the three Techs work together to try to analyze what Beelzie is up to. Thomas suggests round-the-clock monitoring of all NetherWorld frequencies and all Earth communications. Here, Beings don't have to sleep. They never turn their minds off as we do on Earth. There's no mental rest necessary due to an overloaded daily schedule. You know: kids, unreasonable mate, abusive boss, that sort of thing. So the three Techs tirelessly scan the airwaves.

Thomas sets his equipment to record energy peaks. He has a great new receiver, even better than the old one. His old Collins had an "S" meter to measure signal strength. His new EtherKnob has a digital bar-graph that can measure any signal strength. He detects an energy surge emanating from deep in the NetherWorld. His team activates the tracking device that follows the surge. It's headed to Earth, specifically to the Con Edison nuclear power plant in New York, U.S.A. They put the universal translator into action and decode the message. It is a numerical sequence that will speed up the reactor and shut down the entire safety protocol.

One of the Techs, the Security Specialist known as Kiwi, says, "This is bad news. The plant's entire computer system will think it's in shutdown mode and will go offline. Heat from the reactor will rise, and there will be an explosion and meltdown. Millions of people will be harmed."

Thomas readies a counter-message and pinpoints the coordinates. Kiwi calls room 214 and gets the go-ahead. Throughout the EtherWorld, the word GOD! GOD! GOD! is shouted. Thomas collects the burst of energy and beams his counter-message toward the Con Ed plant. He also embeds a safety code to block further messages from the NetherWorld. All the Con Ed control room sees is a self-correcting software blip, and they are not alarmed.

A new Room is set up in Sector C that is the size of four American football fields. Specialists from nearly every science are told to make the Room their home. Thomas is asked to be a temporary member of Room 214's security staff. He is overjoyed.

"Rose, Rose," Thomas summons his Guide.

"I heard. Congratulations. Things are going to get a bit dicey around here. I hope you're prepared for a hard fight. You are not yet blessed with the skill and strength of an Enlightened Being like the rest of us, but you do have a very quirky analytical sense when it comes to signals."

"It's good I can analyze *something*. I'm no damned good with women. I've been in the EtherWorld for seven months and still haven't gotten any nookie."

"Poor baby." Rose hands him a gold mini-star for saving Con Edison.

She then grabs it back from him. "The star was a present for doing good work. I'm taking it back because you are still a Jerk Being."

7

On Earth, unmanned vehicles go into areas that are too dangerous for aircraft or land vehicles. They are called *drones,* and are basically used to destroy other Beings. In the EtherWorld, drones are called *missals.* They are not used to destroy, but to carry messages where outsider Beings are not welcome. There is no formal contact between Rooms 213 and 214. Although Beelzie and Jake are powerful enough to communicate directly, each despises the other, although Jake has pity. They send messages to each other via missals.

These concentrated Supreme Being and NetherWorld messages land in a basket outside their targeted rooms. The last time a message was sent was back in 1931, when Beelzie sent a missal demanding the release and re-entry of a Being from NetherWorld who had asked for asylum in EtherWorld. The Being was successfully purged and admitted into Sector E. She has since been promoted to Sector D. Beelzie demanded her return, but Jake refused, saying that each of them is free to reassign Beings at will, and he approved of her change. There was nothing Beelzie could do. But he is still very angry, and brings up the subject at NetherWorld bourbon suppers. Beelzie is told by a staff member that there's a missal in the basket. He translates.

"There is evidence of unexplained wrongdoing on Earth. A catastrophic event was narrowly averted in New York City, U.S.A. The energy burst that nearly destroyed the nuclear plant there had to have originated in NetherWorld. This is in extreme violation of the Prime Directive. If you continue to embark on this dangerous course, you will start another arms race. I haven't forgotten Eve eating that apple, and Cain and Abel. You had better think twice before doing it again, or your ass is grass."

Beelzie erases the message, and merely writes, "The Devil made me do it, har, har, hardy, har har," and sends the missal back to the Room 214 basket.

There is pandemonium in the NetherWorld banquet hall. All the military hackers are celebrating. Beelzie is unhappy that he wasn't told beforehand what was going on. The last thing he needs is a revolt by the Generals. He shouts, "What the hell do youse guys think this is, the Pentagon? Are you planning some coup, you feeble-brained bunch of tin soldiers? This is my domain! If I'm not told what's going on right now, you will all be tonight's dessert."

The military hackers all laugh and sing, "For he's a jolly good fellow, for he's a jolly good fellow, for he's a jolly good fellowwwwwwwwww, which nobody can deny." Then they all shout *Surprise!* and give Beelzie a hearty round of applause. The lead hacker presents him with a special gift.

They have successfully figured out a way to enter Earth computers and plant a following code that will completely block any other attempts to enter the computer. Since the EtherWorld isn't able to reverse their destruction, they are now free to play.

Beelzie meets with his staff to give them the news. Most are glad, but Hun and Chopper are pouting. "What's wrong with youse guys?" Beelzie asks. Hun says, "I guess computer hacking is okay, drones are okay, high-altitude bombing, cruise missiles, long-range artillery, and tank fire. I guess they're better than the 4-H Club or the Garden Committee, but I'm sad that we no longer go eyeball to eyeball, each facing the other with a small round shield and a three-foot-long sword as sharp as a mother-fucking razor."

"I know, I know, I'm nostalgic too, but we can't do that anymore. What do you think would happen if we told the men, oh yes, and now the servicewomen, from the modern military forces, that they could no longer be electronic specialists or radar operators? What if they had to grab a sword and round shield and chop their enemies' heads off? I'll tell you what would happen. There would be no more wars. It would ruin us. So be thankful there are all these neat ways for modern armies to kill each other without being personal. Robots are the coming thing. It's going to be a real disappointment watching the robots fight each other. Perhaps we can set up a paint-ball device with blood. When a robot is destroyed it could bleed like the real thing."

"It's not the same for me," Chopper says, shedding a tear.

★

"Here's the plan." Beelzie has on his uniform with four rows of shiny gold medals hanging from multicolored ribbons. He is all business, and the Generals are sitting at attention. Half-gallon flasks of red bourbon are at each place, but no one dares to drink until the business is finished.

Beelzie speaks. "There are two species on Earth that are remarkably similar: lemmings and Humans. As you know, lemmings, the dumb little shits, get hairs up their asses and all jump off a cliff at once. Humans do the same thing in many ways. They piss in their own drinking water and foul the air they breathe. Most of our work has already been done for us. The Americans have figured out how to control the weather. This device in Alaska, U.S.A. is called HAARP, Habitation for Alienating American Responsible Programs. We can take a lesson from the Americans on how to lie to the general public. Listen to this."

HAARP is a scientific endeavor aimed at studying the properties and behavior of the ionosphere (the atmosphere's upper layer), with particular emphasis on being able to understand and use it to enhance communications and surveillance systems for both civilian and defense purposes. It will be used to induce a small, localized change in ionospheric temperature so that resulting reactions can be studied by other instruments located either at or close to the HAARP site.

"You have to admit, that is a beautiful load of horseshit. Notice how they even admit that these systems are for both civilian and defense purposes. They even chose letters that are close to AARP, which is a Human geezer group. Surveillance systems, my Satanic Butt. Let me tell you what they really do and what they have done. By the way, I'm looking forward to meeting the people who have designed and created this magnificent machine. They have a great future in the NetherWorld. So, listen to this.

"They have developed a satellite-controlled beam as a mind-control and anti-personnel weapon that works by affecting the Human brain. They have successfully used gasses to create ionospheric holes. They can deliver strong, concentrated energy anywhere on Earth using laser and particle beams. These are as strong as a nuclear weapon. They can cause hurricanes, tsunamis, forest fires, floods, and electrical power failures over areas covering hundreds of square miles. Rumor has it that they caused the earthquake and tsunami in Japan that ruined their nuclear plants. As far as I'm concerned, the men and women of HAARP deserve a round of applause."

Everyone cheers and Beelzie takes a swig of red bourbon. The entire staff does the same thing, and they all slam their tankards down on the table at the same time, except for one General who was a split second late. He was removed from the room and given to the chef to prepare.

Beelzie continues: "We don't have the power to cause a hurricane or an earthquake, but we don't have to. The

Humans have done it for us. All we have to do is use our energy bursts to control the HAARP computers, and we can direct what we want, to wherever we want. It's like an artist's palette. But instead of red, blue, green, and yellow, there's tidal waves, fires, drowned cities, radiation sickness from nuclear contamination, and food and water poisoning, just to name some of the 'colors.' All these wonderful things are now on our palette just waiting for us to mix and use, and we're the ones with the paintbrush. We now have three billion watts of electromagnetic energy we can send on any frequency from 2.5 to 10 megahertz.

"Here's another fact that is working 100 percent in our favor. Our energy bursts, and the energy bursts from the EtherWorld, travel at the exact same speed. Whoever blasts out first has the unbeatable advantage, because a second energy burst can never catch the first. So, we use the Stuxnet virus to target the HAARP software, and then with our new blocking codes, we immediately put up a shield that will repulse any corrective action by Tommy Boy and his pipsqueaks."

"Here's some information for youse guys to whet your appetite. According to human news-wire services, the Japan and Haiti quakes 'show amazing similarities that lead them to believe there's an artificial cause and the use of HAARP technology.' In Haiti, 'low-frequency signals of 2.1 Hz were detected for forty hours before the earthquake occurred,' and in Japan they really stirred the pot. The very same frequency signals were detected for about fifty hours before the earthquake, as well as for several hours afterward.

"They almost got away clean, but a bunch of nosy, mealy-mouthed journalists kept saying it wasn't a natural occurrence but a new manmade weapon. They said that such a low-frequency signal lasting for many hours cannot happen naturally. They were eventually debunked as a bunch of crackpot conspiracy theorists, and nobody cared to listen.

"To HAARP!" Beelzie toasts.

They all take another swig of red bourbon and slam their tankards down on the table. Unfortunately, another General was a beat behind.

★

Jake is speaking at a security briefing. Thomas is sitting in the middle of the table about fifteen chairs away from the head. He has been given special polarized sunglasses so he isn't overwhelmed by Jake's dazzling display. Only those who have reached Enlightenment can view him without sunglasses. Jake speaks.

"Let me tell you about Beelzie. He is a creature of habit. The last three times he did dirty work, it was at precisely 521:42 clock. If he is preparing another energy burst, I'll bet it will be at the exact same time. He's very superstitious. It's up to this security staff to find a way of dealing with it, so please get busy."

521:42 clock was fast approaching. Thomas returns to the Security Room in Sector C. He paces back and forth, up and down, side to side, turns clockwise 360 degrees vertically, 360 degrees horizontally, spins upside-down, rolls counter-clockwise, for a very long time (remember how the astronauts looked when they were weightless in their flight simulator). He doesn't know what to do, and neither do any of the other security personnel. The clock now read 521:37.

Suddenly, Thomas has an idea. He grabs his EtherKnob receiver and redirector and glides quickly to the edge of Sector E, just bordering on Sector F. The Composites are patrolling, and he can smell them. He is that close to the border. At precisely 521:40, Thomas shouts "GOP! GOP! GOP!" All the Beings in the NetherWorld direct their energy toward Thomas, including the Stuxnet virus headed for HAARP. He scans the energy with his analyzer and redirects it harmlessly into Hyperspace. It will be several clocks before they can summon another burst, so he reports back to Room 214. His analyzer is busy decoding the NetherWorld transmission.

Thomas is praised again for his work, but Jake gives a caution. "Beelzie won't make the same mistake twice. He will abandon his superstition of always using 521:42 and will pick another time. He will be ahead of us, so we must prepare an instantaneous response. We must also change our 911 code from D·O·G spelled backward to something new that Beelzie doesn't know. Let's use the word, and I'll spell it backward, Y·O·J. It's up to all of you to quickly get the word out to all Beings in the EtherWorld. Whatever you do, don't say either word or you will tip our hand."

The conversion from D·O·G to Y·O·J was successful. As expected, the NetherWorld did send an energy burst at another time: 519:14. Jake was right and knew what Beelzie would do. At precisely 519:12, Beelzie sent three Composites to the edge of Etherworld and they shouted "GOD! GOD! GOD!" to steal the EtherWorld energy. It was followed by a blast of energy directed again at HAARP. Since the code word had been changed, the NetherWorld could not steal the energy burst from the EtherWorld. EtherWorld retained full power.

Thomas was away from his receiver, but Kiwi saw it and immediately activated the universal loudspeaker "JOY! JOY! JOY!" A micro-clock later a counter-energy beam was directed to chase the NetherWorld beam. Unfortunately, the NetherWorld beam got there first, and a code sequence was instantly entered into the HAARP computers by Beelzie's team. It repulsed the EtherWorld beam. The NetherWorld was now in control of the entire computer system.

The first thing NetherWorld did was create Hurricane Irene. It looked like a classic tropical storm that formed in the usual place, but it was triggered by Beezlie and the NetherWorld. The second calamity they engineered caused torrential rains and flooding in South America. Thousands were left homeless, and there were many deaths. They set up a control room in NetherWorld that was completely hidden and unnamed, so it was cloaked from any EtherWorld scans. Beezlie called the Generals together.

"I'm proud of youse guys. I know, Hun and Chopper, that you are upset that this is pain once removed, and not the sharp pain you like to inflict, but it ain't bad. Now I want the coup de grace. We will decide how to inflict a real beaut of a disaster. We don't want to destroy the Earth, because it would rob us of so much future pleasure. We can, however, create some mayhem that will be truly historical. We will pipe in a live-feed and show it on NetherPanorama. We can charge admission and have a ribald party afterwards. I've got dibs on Diphtheria, she's mine. We set up an orgy hall that is the exact shape and size of the Pentagon in the U.S.A. This is where death will be celebrated for a long time to come."

★

Thomas is inconsolable. He, Rose, and Janis sit at a table in Gabriel's Hideaway. He and Janis both drink too much whiskey, but Rose always keeps a clear head. She looks at Thomas anew. He is no longer the Jerk Being, but possibly the only one in the EtherWorld who can figure out how to counter Beezlie. In an uncharacteristic move she pleads with Thomas to figure something out. Janis has had way too much Southern Comfort and speaks, slightly slurring her words, "Hey, man, it's been over 100 degrees the whole summer in Port Arthur, Texas, and there's been no rain for half a year. There are wildfires everywhere. Fifteen hundred people have lost their homes. That was *my* home, hon. Can you fix this?"

Thomas enters Room Total Peace. He is sitting alone and remembering the times he helped people. He changed the tire for some seniors on the Interstate. He rescued a neighborhood child who was about to run into the path of a speeding car. He counseled a college friend and kept him from committing suicide. He thinks of many things. He thinks, he thinks.

The answer comes to him from his own Being reflected in the Aurora Panorama. *Thinking is energy.* He runs from Room TP back to the Security Room in Sector C. He accesses available data on Human brainwaves and consults with the Enlightened Beings in Security about the wave forms of other Sentient Being brains. He briefs the group.

"The Human brain is an electrochemical organ. It can generate as much as 10 watts of electrical power. It has over 10 billion interconnected nerve cells. If all of them were discharged at once into a single electrode placed on the Human scalp, it would produce as much as 50 millionths of a volt. If you connected a bunch of people in a circuit, you could actually light a flashlight bulb. All this activity is on known frequencies. There are different types of brain waves:
    "Delta waves are between 0-4 Hz. They occur during deep sleep.
    "Theta waves are between 4-7 Hz. This is the twilight zone of reduced stress and conscious awareness.
    "Alpha waves are between 7-12 Hz. They produce relaxation.

"Beta waves are between 13-40 Hz. When we are awake, this is the state we rely on for concentration, alertness. It is the key to all cognition. 40 Hz is the frequency we are after.

"What we need to do is redesign our transmitter to send our energy burst, not to a computer, but directly to the brain of the humans in the HAARP computer control room. They are trying to purge Beelzie's virus, but they can't. Their whole system is in NetherWorld control and can't even be shut down unless they know the code sequence. We can give them that sequence telepathically."

Kiwi advises Thomas that they must consult Room 214. Jake is upset at violating the Prime Directive, but admits that if Beezlie isn't countered soon, more great harm will follow. They have no choice but to intervene. Thomas suggests that the Human may believe the transmission is his or her own thoughts. It's also possible she/he may think it's a voice from someone else in the room, which is not good. He is going to fine-tune the transmission so a minute bit of energy enters the Human's mind directly. He or she will believe it is their original thought.

8

*T*homas hovers above Alaska, U.S.A., trying to pinpoint the coordinates for beaming down telepathic brainwaves to the computer technicians in HAARP. He is capable of selecting an area as small as one square millimeter from anywhere in EtherWorld. It's vitally important that he select the correct person, one who has the ability to cancel the NetherWorld protocols. An energy-burst into the wrong person would be disastrous. For instance, if he selected the person waxing the floors, it would be like telling a Republican politician to appear before his constituents and proclaim his honesty. He would stand at the podium and make a total fool of himself. It just wouldn't work.

While preparations are being made for the transmission, Thomas realizes that he can quickly glide to the upper atmosphere above northern New England, U.S.A. and monitor Cindy's computer. With his newfound knowledge, he can also read her brainwaves, since he knows her exact coordinates. The temptation is too much for him to resist, so he saunters over to the space above Burlington, Vermont, taps into Cindy's brain, and turns the volume up on his EtherKnob receiver so he can read the faint signal.

"I know when I'll do it. When he's at work, I'll hire some worker bees from the temp agency, load all his shit onto a rental truck, and have them taken to a storage facility. I gave Thomas's radio equipment, musical instruments, and computers to Ronald. It bums me out to have them around. I'll be glad when they're gone. When he comes home, the door will be locked, and the locks will be changed. I'd better call the locksmith right away. I'll pay the local sheriff to serve him with divorce papers. Ronald won't know what hit him."

Thomas realizes that Cindy is up to no good as usual and about to trash her husband. The idea of her giving away his priceless possessions to a cipher like Ronald angers him immensely. He wants to send her a telepathic message, *Jump off a bridge, bitch*, but refrains from acting out his hostility. He continues to listen.

"Hello, Ma. Soon, it's a done deal. I'm rid of him for good. Why don't you come over? It's going to be fun watching him when he gets home. Now we can buy that beach house in Tampa. We can have a new bronze-toned boy toy every week and discard them like paper napkins when we've had enough. (Cindy is also prone to bad metaphors.) Listen, the foreign subsidiary royalties are much higher than expected, and *The Princess and the Pauper* is going to be made into a movie. There's mega-bucks from the movie rights. Since I own the name, I'm going to open that strip club in Tampa right near our house, and call it The Princess and the Pauper. I think it's great to have a place right there on the water with pole dancing, gambling, and a little back-room action, if you know what I mean. I've been around dullards all my life. Now it's time for some excitement!"

Thomas is one micro-clock away from beaming down a message telling Cindy to drive her car fast into a concrete bridge abutment, but again he stops himself. He has an important job to do. He glides away from New England, U.S.A. and returns to the space above Alaska, U.S.A. After some painstaking work on minute telemetry, he is able to select and pinpoint the one Human who will receive the energy burst. He returns to Sector C and plots the coordinates into the EtherKnob transmitter. Jake gives the go-ahead. One of the security technicians shouts "JOY! JOY! JOY!" and a huge surge of energy enters the transmitter. Thomas directs it toward the control room at HAARP into the lead technician's brain, who thinks he suddenly got a great idea.

"I've got it! Here's how we can bypass the lockdown. Enter these codes into the system, and then create a new password seventy-five characters long."

With this action, Beelzie and the NetherWorld are thrown out of the HAARP computer. Beelzie was attending the Pentagon orgy when one of his Generals told him the news. He was so riled that he left Diphtheria and half a bottle of red bourbon alone in the Pentagon. He was in no mood for humor. He called all his Generals to the banquet hall.

This time there was no food or drink in front of them. He spoke very quietly and deliberately. "Find a way to duplicate what Thomas," and then Beelzie shouts at the top of his lungs, *"Yes, Thomas that useless wimp!"* He speaks quietly and calmly again, "Find a way to duplicate what he has done. I will give you a little incentive here. There are millions of Beings in Sector T who would love to have your positions. There is no General's union in the NetherWorld. What there is, is, is a very good chef who is going to serve all of youse guys as dessert if you don't produce results." Beezlie shouts again, *"What we have here is the Exxon, Blackwater, Halliburton Protocol! I taught them everything they know. I am almost as powerful as any American corporation. You are all expendable. Now get busy!"*

★

In Sector C Security, Thomas has been working closely with a Sentient Being named Goga from Tkxty, a lone, but very large planet around the Star 37, Geminorum. Since he can't understand his/her speech, Thomas is dependent on the Enlightened Beings in Security to provide him with a translation. Even then, it is difficult for him to grasp. He is working on the third path to Enlightment, Sentient Reciprocity. Progress in this stage is tough to measure because there are no tests. The subject matter is difficult to quantify and qualify because there are so many variables in the Beings themselves. Thomas's Guide, Rose, has the responsibility to decide when he has communicated successfully with other Beings, without translation.

Thomas is very attracted to Goga and asks Kiwi, an Enlightened Security Specialist, whether it is a he or a she.

"Goga is neither male or female, per se. Actually it, for lack of a better word, is both. It depends on the Being it interacts with whether it will be male or female."

"What does Goga look like?"

Kiwi has to think for a few micro-clocks to speak in terms that Thomas will understand. "Goga is about twice your height and three times your width. There is an electrical mass of neurons that sparkle on the outer edge of its left side, and there's a soft, spongy middle about waist high. Its brains—Goga has three—are located in its hands. It uses these hands to supply information to the rest of itself. On the right side, Goga is made primarily of a very elastic, tissue-like substance that can change shape, compress, or expand. Goga is a very tactile being with 117 different pleasure points."

Thomas is intrigued and speaks again to Goga while Kiwi translates. "In your World, do you have families and raise children?"

Kiwi translates. "Reproduction foremost, meeting first, extended coupling, greater pleasure to entice and stay. Formed bond, with bonds from others to strengthen gene pool. Permanent coupling dependent on internal and external harmony."

Thomas doesn't understand but thinks, *Yeah, I like you too, sweetie.* Thomas doesn't realize that Goga can read his thoughts. They shake hands, and Thomas is glad that Goga likes him.

He tells Kiwi that he would like to have sex with Goga, and asks him, somewhat embarrassed, to pop the question for him.

"You just had sex," Kiwi responds, "when you shook hands. Goga found it very pleasurable and wants to know if it was good for you. Goga also wants to know what is *nookie*."

Rose approaches Thomas and offers him a qualified congratulations for his first direct communication with another Sentient Being. "I should have known that you would choose your old familiar subject matter."

"Aw, Rose, why do you tease me so? When can we go to a Swirl together?"

"I have decided that we will go to a Swirl together."

"When! When!"

"The very day you become Enlightened. You need an incentive, Thomas, because you have a Monkey Mind, a very horny Monkey Mind. Now let's get back to understanding Sentient Reciprocity."

★

Jake asks the inhabitants of Sectors A and B to visit the Security Center in Sector C for advanced training in the fine art of telepathic beaming into Human brains. They are instructed first on how to listen to news events and personal cellphone conversations, on how to recognize Evil about to happen, and finally how to plot the coordinates to influence them to the Good.

Thomas figures out that they don't need a tremendous burst of energy from all Beings. He used only a small fraction of that to beam the correction into the mind of the HAARP computer technician. The rest he sent into Deep Space. Only 100 Enlightened Beings are necessary to produce a charge strong enough to read and send messages to anyone on Earth. This is great news to Jake, who is organizing a massive relief effort for the beleaguered Earth. Devolution has been rather constant since the first Human was aware of his own existence. Jake has considered, many times, removing Humans as the dominant species on Earth, and elevating lemmings to Human consciousness. Lemmings would continue to have the problem of overpopulation and so would the Humans. But the Humans would be jumping off cliffs. In many ways, that would be esthetically more pleasing, especially since lemmings don't drive Lincoln Navigators or vote for Republicans.

Thomas readies the first test. One hundred Enlightened beings, specially chosen for this honor, including Rose, are to provide the energy. Kiwi is to send the signal, and Jake himself will choose the Human recipient. Thomas puts on his polarized sunglasses so he can be in the same space with

Jake, and hands him an EtherKnob transmitter with special brainwave enhancer. Jake reads the mind of a street thug in Birmingham, in the United Kingdom. He is about to mug an elderly woman and take her purse. Each group of 100 beings who actually form the heavenly power-supply has its own code for capturing the energy. This group came up with a rather cute code phrase, "One, two, three, GO!" Kiwi sends the message, which Jake composes, to the thug, who is named Rodney.

"She looks just like my mother. She's so old, what could I possibly want in her purse? I can't harm anyone. I'm just angry because I'm poor. I'll get a job tomorrow."

Rodney doesn't attack the woman, who is named Vivian, but instead offers to help her cross the street. She declines, and he wishes her a good evening and tells her to be safe. The entire EtherWorld throws a great party. Gabriel's Hideaway is packed, and Rose has to order more Jameson for the bar.

This scene is repeated over and over, thousands of times per Earth hour, in all parts of the World. Dick Cheney apologizes for water-boarding, George Bush for bankrupting the Treasury, and the Wall Street bankers for their greed. The new Republican Tea Party members of the U.S.A. House of Representatives create a bill for universal health care, while ending foreign wars. They give two billion dollars to National Public Radio.

★

Beezlie is in mourning. He is inconsolable. Every second clock he asks his team what's going on, and whether they can duplicate what Thomas has done. Gone is his swagger and bravado. He acts like a beaten Being.

"I've never seen him like this," Hun says to Chopper. "I gave him a present, a neat live-feed of bankers having sex with pigs, and another great feed of homes being washed away during Hurricane Katrina. All he said was, 'That's nice,' and continued moping. I just can't seem to cheer him up."

Hun proposes to Beelzie a raid into the EtherWorld to capture Thomas and his equipment. "Just like the great battle in the old days."

"Yeah," Beelzie remembers, "but they kicked our asses. We're the Fallen Angels, remember, we were cast out. They are too strong. Our Composites are only tough in the NetherWorld. Get them outside in the EtherWorld, and a mug of warm Guinness stout thrown at them will blow them up. No, we are here and they are there. Our only hope will be if some treacherous genius learns how to put evil thoughts into Human minds, using something other than television. Although, I must say, it did work well in Italy. Berlusconi poisoned the whole country with his TV shows. We know the Evil thoughts are already there; we just have to learn how to intensify and channel them."

Hun and Chopper are not convinced they can't wage and win a successful action against the EtherWorld. Hun has an idea.

"Lookie here, Chopper, we can't take them on Empire to Empire. Shit, neither can terrorist groups win against the huge armed forces of goody-goody countries. Beelzie is from the old school, where two armies formed long lines and proceeded to attack each other. Why, families would picnic on the hillsides, watching them. There have never been such wonderful entertainment spectacles before or since, with the exceptions of gladiator fights in the Roman Coliseum and the debate between Sarah Palin and Joe Biden. I like mass stabbings, choppings, slicing, dicing, mangling, and mincing on a grand scale as much as you do. The grander the better, but we have to be practical. Sometimes we have to settle for a blown-up airliner or suicide bomb. Let's plan a strike into their World to get Thomas and his equipment."

Chopper says, "I don't think that's a good idea. It would start a terrestrial war, and Beelzie will be pissed that we didn't include him in our plans. We could wind up being served as antipasto."

"But that's only if we fail. With all the Good being done on Earth, we may as well be terminated. There's no more pure pain to unleash and experience in the NetherWorld. You wait and see, with no fresh action, all those Beings on the edge of our border will become soft. They will cross over into the EtherWorld's bottom Sector E and ask for asylum and, hot-fires-be-burning! *forgiveness*. Our World will shrink, and all we will be able to do is watch reruns of past gories on NetherPanorama. There will be no more live feeds. Is this what you want?"

"Hell, no," Chopper agrees. "When do we get started?"

"Right now! Here's the plan. Composites are stupid and expendable. When they cross into EtherWorld, they will lose most of their power. But 50 or 100 of them can make quite a bit of noise. This will create a diversion. First, EtherSecurity will detect them and focus energy on the Composites. Security will wait a few clocks because they will wonder whether the Composites have wandered into Sector E by mistake. We will do a 270-degree loop and enter the EtherWorld from the other side. We will have a NetherReceiver with us and, although it is useless here to pick up their energy, it can do a great job once we are in their force-field.

"We will pinpoint where their Communications Central is located. If it's a separate Room, we've got it made. If it's in or close to Room 214, they will get us and we will probably be served as Hunny cake and Chopped meat. We'll take two destructive computer specialists with us to identify the software we need. We grab Thomas and hotfoot it out of there the same way we came in. The Sector A Beings are faster than we are, but we'll have a big head start. Waddaya think?"

★

In the EtherWorld every Being rejoices in the newfound knowledge that they are fighting for the Good on Earth. Jake is still worried because they have totally abandoned the Prime Directive. He suspects that Beezlie won't stay inactive for long. After all, this has been going on since Adam and Eve, or two happily mated, ugly, foul-smelling, three-foot-long hairy lizards, if you subscribe to Charles Darwin's theories. Considering how Humans turned out, Darwin was probably right. For now at least, the atmosphere is truly jovial.

The last time the EtherWorld was this happy was when Franklin Delano Roosevelt created Social Security. Jake decides to keep all the worrying to himself, for now at least, and let everyone have a good time. He proclaims, starting with tomorrow's clock, Game Week. There are competitive and cooperative games and contests throughout all Sectors, except the bottom half of Sector E. The Beings there are very aggressive and tend to be whining spoilsports, much like the New York Yankees. There's a great rivalry between the C and D Sectors. Bragging rights for the last Game Week belong to Sector D. They received the Jake Trophy, and it is proudly displayed above the North bar at Gabriel's Hideaway.

A game is about to begin. It's called Toss the Composites. 2,000 Beings from Sector C and 2,000 from D line up on either side of a playing field that looks like a target with concentric circles. In the center "bull's-eye" is a deep hole with a floral-scented spinning bath of cleansing solution, composed of beautiful poetry read by angelic voices and music played by angelic musicians. Yes, it even includes the much-written-about, and totally cliché harp music from Connemara, Ireland. There's a huge income tax refund, a clean bill of health from a local dentist, and the complete lingerie collections of the Nuns of Saint Andrew's in Glasgow, Scotland.

Composites who have been caught entering Sector E in the past have been saved up for this game. They are now bound tightly in leather straps and reshaped into a ball. Jake isn't too happy about this part of the game, but it really does build an excellent esprit de corps within the teams. The object of the game is to toss a Composite into the center hole of the bull's-eye. A total of ten Composites have been prepared, and each Sector gets to throw five. You are allowed to roll your Composite into the other Sector's Composite to bonk him out of the way. As a matter of fact, this game is affectionately called "Bonk" in the EtherWorld. No team can roll their Composite directly into the bull's-eye; the distance is too great. Composites that are bonked outside the circle are re-tossed. The winning team is the one that successfully bonks the other team's Composites out of play, while at the same time advancing theirs by bonking him into the center hole.

When the winning Composite falls through the bull's-eye, all 50,000 Beings are immediately immersed in the delightful spinning bath. It completely overloads their systems, and they run out, violently shaking their hands and feet, and wiping their eyes, ears, nose, and mouth to get rid of the assault to their senses. When all of them come out shakin' and twitchin', the winning team cheers. It really is quite a sight to watch those Composites scamper, much like a Tea Party Convention that has been exposed to logic and reason. Then both teams send a burst of energy that recaptures the 50,000 individual Beings in the Composite. He is reformed and hurled back into the Netherworld. The other Composites are kept bound, and put back in the sports locker for next time.

The tossed Composite is now contaminated with the contents of the spinning bath. Hun, Chopper, and the rest of the NetherWorld generals see images of Jonathan Livingston Seagull, Hallmark Mother's Day cards, Perry Como records, Kate Smith singing D·O·G Bless America, stuff like that. I don't have to tell you the kind of reception that Composite gets when he returns home. This doesn't bother the Bonk players, but Jake is concerned that perhaps it's a bit sadistic.

The winning team in this clock's Toss the Composites game is again Sector D, and they retain the Jake Trophy.

9

Beelzie and his Bubs don't have a clue how to end the supremacy of EtherWorld and their influence on Earth Beings. Hun and Chopper have logistical problems lining up two military destructive computer specialists who can recognize the software they need to plunder. This delay can't be avoided, but slowly their plans are being refined.

There is a Pax Romana in the AfterWorld. It's like the lull before World War II. They called it the Phony War with neither side initiating hostilities. The lack of conflict has pleased the Beings in EtherWorld. They now turn their energies to other pursuits.

Room PAP, where Thomas is a very welcome visitor, has decided to stage a reality TV show. They chose not to use themselves as participants, since there is so much work necessary to produce and direct. They selected Beings based on the recommendations of Room Head Shrink. If a Being is judged to be not fit to live among his peers, he or she is put in Room ST, Severely Troubled. The people who can't even adjust to that Room are considered perfect for parts on the reality show.

The Beings in Room PAP decide to combine all the reality series on Earth into one dramatic show, and to add a few wrinkles of their own. They will take real events in people's lives and combine them into a potpourri of unanticipated events. They create an outline and distribute it to all the Beings who want to try out for parts. They don't have a script. The actual dialogue and events are unknown, because reality in the future is unknown. They have three fully equipped mobile studios that can be on location in a micro-clock. The soundman is using the same EtherKnob equipment that Thomas used so successfully in his work.

The show is about to begin. As they do on Earth, credits flash on the screen showing the producer, the director, and the names of the participants. We don't say *actors*, because this is reality TV and the people on screen are only being themselves. They would never act differently because a camera was on them. (Right, and Lindsay Lohan has taken vows to become a Carmelite Nun.) Editing is an art on these productions. There are so many camera angles and so much footage, it's difficult to piece it together into a watchable show.

The name of the show is *The Surviving Housewife Apprenticed to a Lunatic Accountant from Pittsburgh.* The show opens with a situation set up by the producers. Six extremely attractive housewives are asked to give up their husbands and cohabitate with horny members of the opposite sex who are also very attractive. They are told to sleep nude in the same bed but are not allowed to initiate any touchy-feely activity. The couple who ignores this rule first, wins the first round. Housewife number three never did get it on. Her inconvenient morality is ridiculed by the staff and all the extras on the set, and she is voted off the show. This scene is disappointing because it lasts only seventeen Earth seconds. Housewife number six is the winner of round one.

The second round is Housewife Survival. The remaining five ordinary Housewives go through their normal day, except the reality people have created special hazards they have to overcome. The first hazard is the youngest child spinning along with blue jeans in the dryer. The second is the family dog crapping on the lasagna that is to be served for dinner. The third is a husband who informs his wife he has just lost his job and is running away to Mexico with his secretary. The fourth is most severe. The Housewife discovers that her lipstick container which reads Cherry Pink is actually Shocking Pink.

Each Housewife is followed through her daily routine by fast, hand-held cameras. Housewife number six takes her shocking pink lipstick and rubs it all over the lasagna to hide the spot where the dog crapped. The close-up camera work adds to the suspense. Will her family come home while she is still rubbing? Can they taste the difference? The camera swoops low as she bends over the lasagna and exposes almost her entire cleavage. She is panting from the excitement and finishes just before her husband Ralph, a lunatic accountant from Pittsburgh, comes home. All looks serene, like a 1950s sitcom. Such a nice family is happily sitting down to their evening meal, but reality TV is very unpredictable.

She whispers in Ralph's ear that she knows of his plans to go to Mexico, and that he just ate dog crap in his lasagna. Only the Housewife, the children, and the rest of the entire Galaxy know what's going on, but this comes as a surprise to the husband. Viewers all over the EtherWorld chortle at his discomfort. The woman who got the most points is the same person who was the first to screw in the previous sequence, number six. Housewife number two cries when she can't get the crap out of the lasagna, and she is voted off the show.

The Housewife Shopping round takes place in a typical American mall in Los Angeles, California, U.S.A. The four remaining Housewives are each given $500 to spend as they wish. A panel of judges will decide which housewife bought the best goods. Winners will be judged on the appropriateness of their purchases, and how many have to be returned.

Housewife number one goes online to Amazon.com and buys durable American-made clothes and jewelry. Housewives two and three are gone. Housewife number four goes to WalMart and buys $500 worth of cheap Chinese clothes. Housewife number five goes to WalMart and buys $500 worth of cheap lead-painted Chinese toys and contaminated sheetrock. Housewife number six goes to WalMart and buys $500 worth of toasters, mixers, and other appliances made in China that only last a few hours before they break down. Since number six had the most returns, once again she is declared the winner. The first Housewife is voted off the show by the judges because she is abnormal and unrealistic. That leaves only Housewives four, five, and six remaining.

The best part of the show is the Challenge round. The contestants are placed in situations they have never encountered before and are judged on their ability to adapt and take control of the scene. Housewife number four is a blonde riding on her bicycle. She sees three huge alligators on the path directly in front of her, ready to lunge. All she has in the wicker basket on her handlebars is a bouquet of flowers. She has to make a quick choice: Does she go forward or does she turn around? Naturally, she pedals toward the alligators. The flowers will be used for her services. What's left of her is shoveled off the show, leaving only Housewives five and six.

The last round, to decide the winner, uses a creative split-screen to show Housewives five and six simultaneously. On the left side of the screen, we see Housewife number five sitting in a restaurant. The waiter brings her a bowl of soup. In the soup she sees horrible maggots and creepy-crawlies swimming around. In this part of the Galaxy, to refuse to eat food is punishable by instant death. She asks the waiter for some NetherNog, and when no one is looking she spills the soup into the potted plant near her table. The judges are impressed with this quick-thinking action. The waiter brings the NetherNog, but unfortunately it has the same maggots and creepy-crawlies swimming around. Number five can't ask the waiter for any more food, because she knows it will be awful. The entire kitchen staff is now standing around her holding knives and meat cleavers. She throws the

NetherNog into the waiter's face and makes a break for the door. She gets out okay.

At same time she is running out the restaurant door, the sixth housewife gets a chance to show her adaptability. She is placed in the Chamber of the House of Representatives, U.S.A. She has a cage full of skunks. She is told to open the cage door when a Congressman says something stupid. The judges will decide if her timing is good or bad. When John Boehner, Speaker of the House, calls everyone to order, she lets the skunks out. She acted in *anticipation* of his saying something stupid. The skunks recognize kindred spirits and jump into the laps of the Tea Party freshmen Representatives. This creative foresight earns her another win, and a clean sweep in...

The Surviving Housewife Apprenticed to a Lunatic Accountant from Pittsburgh!

The show receives mostly negative reviews from *Variety Magazine,* but they give Housewife number six a Best Newcomer Attagirl. She is told by Sector B that when Italian premier Berlusconi passes on, she can be his Guide, even though she has the morals of an alley cat. If he doesn't end up in the NetherWorld, she will probably have a high position in his cabinet. Here's the complete review from *Variety*:

"Room PAP has produced a new reality TV show, *The Surviving Housewife Apprenticed to a Lunatic Accountant from Pittsburgh.* It sucks. Hey, don't badmouth us for making fun of them. We don't think it's very funny. But what is absolutely fucking hysterical is the fact that you extraterrestrial nincompoops are actually watching this shit.

"Are your own lives so boring and mundane that you have to watch someone else doing the things you should be doing? Do you play music or just turn up your iPod? Do you make love, or just watch X-rated movies? Do you know how to cook or do you watch these 'killer' chefs compete against each other? Do you watch, sitting there in a media-induced alpha state, while some human garbage disposal scarfs down thirty-five pounds of cheesecake? Get a fucking life, you are acting like the stupid Americans! We disagree with the judges. The only bright spot in the show was Housewife number five throwing maggot soup into the waiter's face. She should have thrown it in the producer's face. Avoid this show."

Jake sends everyone in Room PAP a message. They are told they have been redirected to a place at the bottom of Sector E, just before the border with NetherWorld. He is not happy. Across the border, Composites are gliding back and forth trying to tune in signals from the rebroadcast of *The Surviving Housewife Apprenticed to a Lunatic Accountant from Pittsburgh* on their NetherReceivers. It seems the show is popular there.

★

Speaking of the NetherWorld, our fearless gay blades, Hun and Chopper, have finished their pre-raid preparations and are ready to blast off for EtherWorld. They are glad that Room PAP has been moved to the edge of the Sector. That part of Sector E is very much in the minds of the EtherFolk, because Jake demoted the entire Room due to that horrible show. A raid by 100 Composites will be directed precisely at the exact point where the new Room PAP has been placed. Room 214 Security will think it's some kind of attempt by horny Composites to plunder room PAP and kidnap the reality-TV Housewives. Security will focus its energy into that sector.

A cracked team of four NetherWorld specialists is ready to put the plan into action. Beelzie was told the day before about the proposal and, although he is depressed, he reluctantly gave the go-ahead. At 924.42 clock the order was given. Hun shouts, "GOP! GOP! GOP!" and 100 Composites charge into Sector E of the EtherWorld. At the same time, the four raiders do a 270-degree loop and enter Sector C by the back door. They guessed correctly. Their scanners tell them the Security Center is in Room MR. Their cloaking devices will last only a short while, so they must work quickly to avoid detection. Thomas and the rest of the staff are watching a review of *The Surviving Housewife Apprenticed to a Lunatic Accountant from Pittsburgh* by the Room 214 Censor Committee. They liked only Housewife number one, when she bought the American-made goods.

"Don't anybody move!" Hun shouts, holding two symbolic razor-sharp Maximus Gladiator Swords. The Security Committee has never encountered Evil directly in front of them before, but Thomas has seen it firsthand.

"So, wimp, you have some information for us. Get your EtherKnob and software, you're going for a ride."

"You know these guys?" Kiwi asks Thomas.

"Sweetie the Hon is an old friend of mine."

The Hun clangs his swords together and places one on each of Thomas's shoulders in a threatening move to cut off his head.

"You won't do it, Hon, you need me."

"Don't spell it that way. I'm warning you, it's HUN!
"HON!"
"HUN!"
"HON!"
"HUN!"
"HON!"
"HUN!"
This scintillating back-and-forth dialogue continues for about five Earth minutes. Thomas is very clever in delaying the raiding party. Their cloaking devices have worn off and their smelly insides are now visible to all.

"Nuts, Hun, we've been exposed," Chopper exclaims. "Perhaps we should leave now."

They grab Thomas as a hostage, along with the secret protocols and codes for Human mind communication, and

125

hotfoot it out of Sector C. They leave the way they came in, via the back door.

The JOY alarm had already been sounded when the Composites invaded Sector E, so there is no energy available to stop the raiding party. Hun and Chopper cross into the NetherWorld, place Thomas in a Containment Room, and bring his equipment into the Decipher Room. Thomas tries to access Room TP but is unable to do so from deep within his cell. *Why didn't I think of Room TP before, when they were kidnapping me out of the Sector? Rose would have remembered. I can't wait to become Enlightened.*

Thomas has a plan. They need him to fine-tune the codes to pinpoint exact Human locations. They could do it themselves, but it would take a very long time. They will have to release him from the Containment Room.

Two of Hun's surrogate sweeties grab Thomas and attempt to bring him to Beezlie. He tries again to access Room TP but is too far away. He has to be someplace in the EtherWorld. He thinks quickly. Enough time has passed for the NetherWorld to recharge its stored energy. He knows their code from the legends Jake tells. He shouts "GOP! GOP! GOP!" and all the NetherWorld Beings send their energy directly to him.

He piggybacks on the energy and beams into a Composite Being that is headed into the EtherWorld to reinforce the invaders, who are being badly defeated. He now shares space in this Being with some of the worst people in human history. His presence is contaminating the others. Like a rotten apple, he is rubbing off on the Evil Beings (Thomas is also prone to clichés) and making them Good. As soon as the Composite crosses into the EtherWorld, Thomas accesses Room TP, and Jake immediately allows his passage. The watered-down Composite limps back home.

Thomas is taken to Room 214 for a debriefing. Rose is there and gives him a non-sexual hug.

"That was a creative way to get back into EtherWorld. I suppose they now have all the equipment and codes necessary to do their dirty work?"

"I didn't give them the codes, but they will figure them out eventually. They won't be as accurate as we are. We can beam energy down to a spot that is one millimeter square. I estimate their capabilities at about three square meters, maximum, even when they figure out how to coordinate the X and Y axes. This may seem good enough, but in a crowded room, they can easily send energy to the wrong person."

Thomas badly needs to unwind. He glides to Gabriel's Hideaway, and this time sits at the South bar. He spots George Washington drinking a cherry coke with vodka.

"Mister First President, I barely recognized you, sir, without your white wig. My name is Thomas, and I always wanted to ask you, is that cherry-tree incident really true, or is it the stuff of legend?"

"What is a president, Thomas?"

"A leader, sir?"

"Yes, but he's also something else. He's a politician. Politicians lie; that is in their DNA. If I had cut down that cherry tree and my old man caught me, I would have blamed it on my sister. Do you know what really bothers me? I'll tell you, son. Ben Franklin is on the 100-dollar-bill, Jackson is on the 20, and Hamilton is on the 10. Grover Cleveland got his mug on the 1,000. How did he rate the 1,000-dollar-bill? Where did they put me? On a stinkin' 1-dollar-bill. That really hurts."

"Sorry, sir."

10

$\mathcal{G}$abriel's isn't crowded. Thomas notices an interesting-looking Being sitting in the middle of the South bar. He introduces himself. "Hello, my name is Thomas Buchetta. I see you are reading a book about astronomy."

"Pleased to meet you, Thomas. My name is Eugene Weslen Roddenberry. Most people call me Gene."

"Wow! You're the guy who created *Star Trek*!" Thomas is very excited. "Please tell me all about yourself. That was always my favorite show. When I was a teenager I was a bona fide Trekkie. Where are you living now?"

"I live in Sector B. I guess I should start at the beginning. I was born August 19, 1921 and died October 24, 1991. I was blessed to live the kind of life I dreamed of. I was a World War II flier with 89 combat missions, and later worked as a commercial pilot. I was a cop for a while with the Los Angeles Police Department. I supported my family while I wrote scripts and screenplays. The world I created spawned six television series, 715 episodes, and twelve films."

"It's such an honor to be sitting here with you, Gene. You coined terms like Prime Directive, Cloaking Device, Warp Drive, Star Date, "Beam me up, Scottie," and many others that have become a part of all science fiction Space odysseys."

"Thanks, Thomas. I'm proud that I was one of the first Humans to have his ashes sent into Space. They are preserved here in EtherWorld. I consider my works morality plays, the classic battle between Good and Evil. It still rages on."

Thomas and Gene talk for hours. Thomas finally leaves Gabriel's and seeks out Rose, who is gliding near Sector B.

"Rose?"

"What is it, Thomas?

"I've been in the EtherWorld for almost eight Earth months and I haven't eaten anything. I suddenly remembered food. I'm famished."

"Mmmmm," Rose is troubled.

"What's the matter?"

"I have to admit something. I was selfish. Do you remember when I was promoted and Room 214 threw a party for me? We had some great pastries. I should have saved you some cannoli."

"You had cannoli? You had cannoli? Where can *I* get cannoli?"

"I don't know, Thomas. Jake provided the refreshments, and it would have been gauche and impolite to ask from where."

"You know, Rose, I did all the cooking at our house. Cindy was totally useless in the kitchen. Her one job was to wash the car, and that was because she could take it to the car wash. If I didn't cook or clean the bathroom, we would have lived in muck and starved to death. I feel sorry for that poor bastard she married. He should count himself lucky she wants a divorce. She's moving in with her Mommy because Mommy will do all the work. She's rich enough to afford permanent staff. She can have cooks, maids, and gardeners, but she's too cheap to part with her millions. What a bitch! But I digress, we were talking about food."

"Thomas, what is it going to take for you to stop giving her the power to torment you? She is making her own Hell on Earth. She is totally out of your control. You should send positive vibes to her so she changes, or we both know where she may end up."

"Thanks, Rose. I'll be back later."

Thomas glides to Room L, the Library, and checks all the listings for restaurants. He is very surprised to see that there are only a few thousand places with Memory Meals. He surmises that food isn't very important here. *I suppose every Being is more concerned with food for the Soul. But that has its limits. I'm hungry, and not for knowledge. Unfortunately, there are no menus in the Library listings.* He selects Mag's Place, which sounds like it could have some good home cooking.

An interesting fact about the restaurants, which Thomas didn't know until today, is that they are not within any particular Sector. The people who run them, and eat in them, are from every Sector. The restaurants themselves are in Free Space. He glides to Mag's Place and sits down at a crude wooden table, with a seat made from a wooden board that has been placed between two large rocks. A rather homely, but pleasant, woman brings him the menu. He asks her if she is serving lunch or dinner.

"We call dinner EveGrub here, Mr. Thomas. That's all we serve. Here's the menu."

Thomas looks it over. Fish, seal, mammoth, sea birds, shellfish, seaweed, eel, and pike are the foods listed. On the back of the menu is a brief history of Mag's place.

"Mag's place is the oldest restaurant in the EtherWorld, founded by Mag Grub 35,000 years ago. She is a proud member of the Cro-Magnon family of Humans. Her family originated in the Middle East and wandered into France. She did not learn her cooking techniques, however, from Julia Child, or get her dessert menu from Austrian pastry chefs. She doesn't have a dessert menu, but recommends grubs, since they are tasty. She was affectionately named after that delicacy. Her people lived in caves or by the sea. It is that rich ancient tradition that Mag Grub is proud to continue."

Thomas couldn't finish his meal. As a matter of fact, he couldn't even start it. *I have to ask Bill Buckley where to find a good restaurant. I can't continue to experiment like this.*

"I haven't given it much thought, Thomas," Bill says. "I've been reading the *National Review* and working on my memoirs. You know, Thomas, I founded that magazine in 1955. I hosted over 1,400 *Firing Line* episodes, wrote all manner of books, a plethora of syndicated newspaper articles, but the one thing I regret is not being on *Real Housewives*. If you find a good restaurant, let me know. We can bring Joe with us."

"That's a good idea, Bill. The only food at Gabriel's Hideaway is peanuts, and most of them have been crushed by General Patton and Lenin."

Thomas is convinced that very few people eat any Virtual Food in the EtherWorld. He returns to the Room L listings and spots Cleo's Palace.

"What the hell, I'll give it a try."

He wonders if Cleo might be a shortened form of Cleopatra, and is concerned that he could get a menu of ancient Egyptian food. Sure enough, when he opens the door, Cleo is indeed Cleopatra.

"Thomas, I haven't seen you since you were bounced out of Room W by the Virgin Mary. How are you getting along?" She doesn't wait for him to answer. "That's good, honey. Look, I got to run. Hope you enjoy your meal. I selected the absolute best and most faithful of my family slaves to run this place, and I know you won't be disappointed."

He reads the restaurant's history, which is in big letters on page one of the menu. It says nothing about the food, but describes Cleopatra in every minute detail. Her height is listed at five-feet-ten, without heels, and her measurements at 40-26-38. He opens the menu and reads the selections: ox-flesh, hard-bread, sweet-oil, fat, honey, figs, and vegetables in season. Thomas selects a plate of vegetables, but he doesn't recognize any of them, and is not pleased that they are raw.

He glides back to Room L for one last attempt at finding a decent place. He chooses The Forum. Perhaps it has Roman or Italian roots, and he can sample cuisine that his ancestors would have eaten. The food is probably awful, but at least he will learn something. *Food for thought*, he quips to himself.

The Forum is a lavish place with frescoes on the walls and fountains at all four corners. He was right, this is indeed a Roman restaurant. The menu is actually broken down into Breakfast, Lunch, and Dinner. For breakfast you can choose salted bread, wine, dried fruit, eggs (they don't say what kind) and milk (they don't say what kind). The lunch menu is salted bread, fruit, salad, meat or fish (they don't say what kind). For dinner he can choose among onions, porridge, pancakes, meat (again, who knows?), eggs, and fruit. He could also have sea urchins, mussels, or oysters. Thomas appreciates the basket that is placed on his table. It contains figs, nuts, pears, apples, grapes, cakes, and honey. The basket looks clean. He is afraid to sample anything on the menu because there are too many unknowns. *This is a little better, but still not what I'm after.* He orders a glass of wine and eats everything in the basket.

Thomas does find a great Chinese restaurant. It's open every day, even during festivals and holidays. The food is excellent and the waitstaff are friendly. It is very crowded and noisy, but he hasn't found a better place to eat. He is really surprised, with all the Italians who have passed on, that there are no Italian restaurants in the EtherWorld.

He has an idea. Sentient Beings in some Galaxies can multi-task to accomplish about 40,000 things simultaneously. As he travels along the path to becoming an Enlightened Being, he finds he is able to do two things at once. He is fully committed to devoting himself to security, but he has extra unused energy (please don't ask him what kind) he could devote to opening an Italian Restaurant.

"Rose, I have an idea. I can't find a good Italian restaurant here and would like to open one. I'm going to call it Ristoranti Buchetta. I don't know how to go about it, because all the restaurants are in Free Space. Who do I ask for permission?"

"It has to come from the Minister of Gastronomical Delights, who is part of the Room 214 Staff. We call him Gas. He's a neat guy who *loves* to see new restaurants open. I'll bet your idea is a shoo-in. Where will you get your staff?"

"Are you kidding? Do you have any idea how many dead Italian housewives are in the EtherWorld? Each one of them insists she is the best cook. Each one makes the best meatballs, the best lasagna, the best zeppoli. There's a goldmine here waiting to be tapped. The best part is I no longer have to worry about cholesterol."

"Sounds dangerous to me, Thomas. How will you get them to work together?"

"Simple, all I have to do is select an Italian housewife and her mother-in-law, who is also Italian. They always try to outdo each other. The food will be fabulous."

"You'd better treat them well, or they might try to poison you. Remember Catherine de Medici."

★

Rose asks Thomas to meet her in the middle of Free Space, between Sectors A and B.

"The third part of your path to Enlightenment is Sentient Reciprocity. You have communicated successfully with a Being in this Galaxy, but he-and-she was visiting *us*. I remember your giving the Being a new appreciation for the word *nookie*. Now it's time for you to ride the SlingShot and visit another Galaxy."

"Will you be coming with me?" Thomas asks nervously.

"No, you must do this on your own. Let me tell you where you're going. Your next stop is the Andromeda Galaxy, also known as M31, since it's the 31st object on Messier's list of diffuse sky objects. Using Earth as your reference point, it's about 2,000,000 light-years away. As you know, the speed of light is very slow. People on Earth, first made aware of the fact by Albert Einstein, know of no faster method of travel.

"Do you remember when you asked me about how the Universe originated? I told you there were parallel Universes in other dimensions. Earth Humans have a theory. They are close, but didn't get it completely right. They base their theory on negative matter. By compressing the space in front of you and expanding the space behind you, you can ride on a surge-wave of Warped Space. They theorize it could possibly be done through a worm-hole, which may or may not be stable. They are right about the compression and expansion, but it doesn't occur in the same dimension. The SlingShot acts like an abstraction; it runs parallel to our own energy. Think of a turtle, moving along at a snail's pace. I guess that should be a snail, moving at a snail's pace. Right next to it, there's a rocket ship traveling at

25,000 miles per hour. The speed of light is like that snail, and the SlingShot propels us like the rocket, via a parallel Universe."

"What's in this parallel Universe?"

"There are some Rest Areas, but they are not very clean. There's a Welcome Center as soon as you cross into Andromeda. You will encounter some traffic at rush hour, but the delays aren't too long."

"How do you know all this stuff? Most women don't have a clue how their flashlight works."

"You sexist pig!"

"Just kidding, Rose. Don't Enlightened Beings have a sense of humor?"

"Let's get back to my explanation, because your life may depend on it."

"Life? How can that be? I'm already dead."

"Don't Jerk Beings have a sense of humor?"

"Sheesh!" Thomas throws out his arms in exasperation. "Always so serious."

"Andromeda is a Spiral Galaxy with two nuclei. You will be traveling at what Earth Humans call 'warp speed.' If you decelerate the SlingShot too soon, you will have to manually glide to the point where you can return. This will take approximately 2,000 years. If you decelerate too late, since you are moving so fast, you will run directly into the energy of the Spiral Galaxy. You will be spun by centrifugal force 2,000,000 light-years away."

"Can I get an incomplete in this course, and sign up for another? How many Beings and SlingShots have you lost?"

"There are more than a few floating around out there, but eventually they will return, unless they emigrate to another system. There are some theories about how Jake and Beelzie wound up here. They could have originated from someplace else, via some primordial SlingShot."

"You mean that somebody created *Them*?"

"No, They have always existed. There are other Supreme Beings who have always existed."

"Holy Spumoni! Now I have to contend with a bunch of different Gods. Oooops, I forgot. No, wait, it's safe to say that word now because....er....Y·O·J replaced it."

"There are so many things you will learn on your path to Enlightenment. On Earth, Man was considered a higher life form when he achieved a consciousness of his own existence. A rabbit doesn't stop to think that it is a Rabbit Being that was born and that will die. He's happy eating clover and the neighbor's carrots. Man has evolved to be able to produce a complex series of thoughts, to use tools, to formulate abstract ideas, and create a complex society. In the AfterWorld there are many kinds of Beings. There are Lima Beings, Pole Beings, Kidney Beings, and String Beings. They all have a place in the Universe.

"Here's where it gets interesting, and here is your challenge. There are life forms, I can't call them Beings, as you will soon hear, that have a far greater intelligence than the smartest Human. They have also created a technical world that no science-fiction writer on Earth could ever have imagined. However, they have no consciousness of their own existence. Your job is to contact one of these life forms and get him or her to acknowledge your presence.

"That's the easy part. You then have to inspire them to tell you something about themselves. They have no perception of their own existence. You must find a way to hold up a symbolic mirror, so they can see their own reflection. If you complete this assignment successfully, they will become Beings, and you will have completed the third step, Sentient Reciprocity. The instructions on how to operate the SlingShot are on the dashboard. It's very easy."

Rose gives him a non-sexual hug, but also, for the first time, a non-sexual kiss on the cheek.

"I hate it when you tease me!" Thomas shouts as Rose glides away.

He is thinking this assignment is much too heavy for a book of humor. He is deep in thought as he steps into an egg-shaped pod. It is made entirely of glass or some sort of see-through material. The control panel is exactly the same as the dashboard of his 1994 Ford Mustang. It was his favorite car. How did it get into the SlingShot pod? *Of course, they* _know_ *it was my favorite car. I'll bet everyone has a different control panel.*

The instructions are simple. There's a shift-knob on the right, next to the seat. It has a "W" position, for Warp, a "D" position for Decelerate, and an "S" position for Stop. There are two cup-holders in the center console, and one holds a can of Hires Root Beer with ice. He takes a swig, burps, and puts the SlingShot in W.

After about thirty Earth minutes, instructions flash on the dashboard where the tachometer would normally sit. "When you see the Andromeda Spiral Galaxy in the center of your windshield, in the square space that is outlined, put your vehicle in D." Nothing could be easier, and he was wondering why some Beings failed to follow the instructions. Then he remembers what the average SUV driver in America was like.

There's a toll booth one light-year into the Galaxy, and he is instructed to hand the life form a banana. The reasons are complex, and he doesn't want to know them. There are thousands of planets from which to choose, but he has an idea. Perhaps the toll-taker is a life form that doesn't know of its existence. In fact, Thomas is about to encounter a highly evolved, but somewhat mechanical, life form or Being. Of course, he doesn't know which. He lifts up the SlingShot canopy.

"Hello, my name is Thomas, and this is the first time I'm visiting Andromeda."

"Welcome, Thomas."

"Thanks, friend. What is your name?"

"Thomas."

"No, that is what you replied to me when I said it was my first time in your Galaxy. You said, 'Welcome, Thomas.' What is *your* name?"

"Thomas."

"No, *my* name is Thomas. Do you have a name?"

"Welcome Thomas. That is my name. You just gave it to me. I am now a Being. Thank you, Thomas, and thank you for the banana."

"Whoa!" he says out loud. "That was easy." Thomas cruises around for a while and spots a restaurant of some kind just off the freeway. The "food" is all different-colored light beams. Patrons are lying on what look like sofa beds, absorbing the lights, making cooing sounds while they rub against each other. In this part of the Galaxy, sex and food are combined. Thomas is built differently and is upset that he can't participate. He glides back to the SlingShot to finish his Hires Root Beer. A McDonalds Big Mac and sweet potato fries have been left for him.

Thomas decelerates upon entering EtherWorld, and stops at the Border Patrol Station. A uniformed Homeland Security Guard makes him open the SlingShot canopy. He searches inside the discarded hamburger wrapper, and his police dog sniffs it for drugs. The dog growls at Thomas for not sharing the meat.

"I have a few questions for you sir, before you are allowed re-entry.

"Where is your place of Birth?
"Are you a citizen of that Sector?
"How long will you be staying?
"What is your destination?
"Are you a member of any known terrorist organization?
"Are you a member of any unknown terrorist
 organization?
"How large is your penis?
"How many times a week did you have sex with your wife?
"Will you take off your shoes and socks, please? If you
 have toe jam, I must fill out a report.
"Will you agree to a full body-scan, with body-cavity
 probes? We use latex gloves now, sir, because of the new
 rules suggested by our *forceful* Democratic President.
"Will you agree to be hypnotized and questioned while in
 a drug-induced coma?

"Do you support our military-corporate oligarchy?"

Thomas doesn't answer any of the questions. He gives the Guard the finger, and blasts through the border crossing gate, leaving rubber with his eight-cylinder Mustang SlingShot.

11

Thomas is informed that he must pay for the gate he destroyed at the border crossing. The money is to come out of his first week's receipts for Ristoranti Buchetta. He wished he could keep the Mustang SlingShot, but it belongs to all the Beings in EtherWorld.

★

Cindy and her mother, Piranha, rented their Vermont home in the hill section of Stowe for the winter. They bought an 8,000-square-foot villa on the water near Apollo Beach in Tampa. Exactly one mile from the house, there was a foreclosure sale on a waterfront restaurant that went out of business. She purchased this property as well, and made plans for a total renovation. Because Thomas Buchetta's book is still number one on *The New York Times* best-seller list, as his widow, she becomes an instant celebrity. She appears on talk shows, both on radio and online, and even does TV specials. Here is her latest interview, recorded yesterday.

"I feel so much a part of this book. Thomas told me I was his inspiration, but few people know I gave him most of the ideas. He was better at writing than I am, and he was fabulous at transcribing what I dictated. I'm planning a second book, as soon as I find a nice bronze-toned ghostwriter. I'm going to base it on life in my new club, which is nearing completion. As a tribute to my poor late husband, I'm naming my club The Princess and the Pauper. So, back to my book. I'm going to call it *From Pole to Pole*, in honor of the young lovelies who entertain politicians and businessmen who eagerly visit. It's very convenient that the BaySide Motel is in walking distance of my club. I can tell you for a fact, they will have a heap of business. BaySide will owe me big-time.

"By the way, I'm not going to just buy big houses, fancy clubs, and expensive yachts. No sir, I believe in public service, and in caring for my fellow man. I'm going to turn my club into a community dance studio. In the mornings it will be used to teach six-year-old girls pole-dancing. The younger they start, the better they'll be when they reach puberty."

★

NetherWorld Beings have been at work, feverishly trying to piece together the codes that will allow them to beam messages into Human minds.

"I know how they are in the EtherWorld," Beelzie says with assurance. "If there's no conflict, they get complacent and soft. They play all manner of silly games, and dine in fine restaurants, and attend concerts. Did you see that poor Composite that they threw back into our World? They used the noble creature for one of their games and contaminated him beyond repair. I had to give all 50,000 Beings to the chef. I believe they are on tonight's menu. The EtherWorld will pay for this. When we capture one of their Archangels crossing the border, we'll bind him in leather straps and play our own game. We will take archery practice and shoot the wimp with hot-pointed arrows. Into every arrow hole, we'll stuff anchovies and sauerkraut. Then we'll hurl him back. I dare *their* chef to prepare him. He will taste like shit."

There is a problem that NetherWorld technicians can't as yet overcome. They finally succeed in receiving thoughts from Humans, but they are only negative, Evil thoughts. The Humans who have them are already well on the path to the NetherWorld, and don't need Beelzie's help. So far, they have been unable to read any positive, happy, or Humanistic thoughts. It overloads their equipment, which doesn't recognize happiness.

Beelzie's Bubs launch a test energy-beam into a Human in Lisbon, Portugal. They badly miss the target, and the beam lands in a field twenty miles away. It enters a cow. She goes udderly mad, runs down the road, and is never seen again. They have much work to do if they want to turn Good people into Bad. They may have to settle for turning Bad people into Worse, if they can modify the NetherTransmitter to provide the needed accuracy. These modified Humans can then run for the U.S. Senate as Republicans.

★

147

Rose and Thomas are in Free Space, a few blinks away from Room 214.

"The next step on your path to Enlightenment is Universal Awareness. You must be able to send Love to all beings, and receive Love from all beings. I don't mean sex, Thomas, so get that out of your mind before we even start, is that clear?"

"How can you separate the two? Rose, are you saying that you are either in love, or you can have sex, but you can't have sex with someone you love? I don't get it."

"The average semi-civilized person can successfully combine the two. But in many ways you are still a Jerk Being. The very first question you think of, when you meet any type, shape, or form of Sentient Being is what do they look like under their clothes. So, in your case, you have to work on Love as a separate force, independent of physical contact. So far, at least, you have proven that you are incapable of feeling and displaying it. Am I getting through to you?"

"No!"

"Too bad, sorry to hear it. Your first assignment for the Universal Awareness stage is to adopt a pet. I put in a special requisition for you. As you know, that cat you betrayed by squirting him with your hose has left a very bad memory. You attempted to purge it in Room Total Peace, but I suspect the guilt still lingers."

"Not much. He was crapping in my garden and digging up my tomato seedlings."

"As you know, your neighbor's cat was named Boots, a white cat with black feet and a black tip on his tail."

"How did you know that? No wait, I forgot, you know everything." Thomas waves his arms in exasperation.

"Boots died five years ago and is now in EtherWorld. He has been assigned to you as your special companion."

"Great, I guess this is the only pussy I will get here."

"What did you say?"

"Never mind."

Rose and Thomas glide over to Room AS, the Animal Shelter, and Boots is waiting for them in the adoption room. When Boots sees Thomas he arches his back, puffs up his tail, and hisses at him. When Thomas reaches down to pet him, Boots scratches him on the back of his hand.

Rose leaves the adoption room and the Animal Shelter. "Bye for now, I'll let you two get acquainted."

"Nice Bootsy, Bootsy, here kitty, kitty." Thomas bends down on one knee but the cat stands there glaring at him. He again puffs up his tail and arches his back. "Look Boots, don't you want to meet other pussy cats in Free Space?

There are some neat tabbies hanging around The Forum Restaurant. A cute little orange number let me pet her. Do you want to stay in a cage in the Animal Shelter forever?"

Boots purrs and rubs against Thomas's legs. He says mar ow, mar ow, mar ow, and jumps onto Thomas's shoulder.

"Ouch! Try to do that with your claws retracted from now on. Okay, let's go exploring."

Thomas has a new friend. The two Tom cats set out on their grand adventure.

★

Rose continues to expose Thomas to new material, in the hopes of awakening the Love that she knows is inside him. She takes him to Room HYPO, Room Hypochondriac. This is an annex to Room Head Shrink. The Beings are all fit and well, but they imagine they are sick.

"Thomas, as you know, in the AfterWorld you no longer have to worry about your cholesterol. You can't get sick and die because dead you already are. There were people on Earth who were only happy when they talked about sickness and death. They had a permanent negative aura about them. When they came into an Earth room, they would instantly bring everyone down. The worst thing you could have done was ask them how they were. They were always ready to pounce, like a hungry leopard sitting in a tree, at the poor soul who dared ask them that question. The listener would then be subjected to a litany (an Earth quip is 'organ recital') of whatever was, is, or could ever possibly be wrong with them.

"I want you to meet some of these Beings. Your job is to understand why they feel the way they do, and offer Love and Compassion.

"Thomas, this is Dolores. Dolores, this is Thomas." Thomas shakes Dolores's hand.

"Ow, not my hand, my arthritis."

"Sorry, Dolores. I'll shake your foot."

"Ow, not my foot! I have it there, too."

"Perhaps we could rub belly buttons?"

"Thomas!" Rose shouts at him.

"Is there anything I can do to make you happy?" Thomas asks Dolores. "Would you like to eat out, or take in a concert?"

"You can do one thing, if you have a few days. Let me tell you what's wrong with me."

Thomas agrees.

"I have cancer, cataracts, catatonia, diabetes, an eye infection, excess nose hair, my ears are growing, I need a knee replacement and my fanny lifted. All my inner parts are sagging, and my outer parts are sagging even worse....."

Thomas listens patiently to Dolores for three straight days. He finally realizes what is going on. She has memorized the entire diagnostic encyclopedia in the Harvard Medical School Library. She is basically a sadist, who uses her supposed illnesses to torment anyone who will listen. *Rose isn't aware of this. She thinks Dolores is just cranky and in need of cheering up.* He is now between a rock and a hard place. (He still thinks in clichés.)

"Dolores, I have an idea. Why don't I bring you the Medical Encyclopedia of Treatments and you can memorize it. When I visit you next time, I will mention a disease, and you mention the treatment I need to make me well. This will make us both feel better."

"Never, you pervert! Feeling well is for well people, not sick people. What's wrong with you, Jerk?"

"I guess I'm not well."

"Now you're talking. Want to see a movie?"

The next day Thomas glides to Room HYPO and picks up Dolores in Janis's Mercedes, which she let him borrow. They attend the Asteroid Belt Cinema. The screen is huge, and has recently been adapted for EtherScope. Tonight they're showing *The Monster That Ate San Diego, California, U.S.A.* Thomas doesn't remember the film and asks Dolores when it was shown on Earth.

"It wasn't. It's locally produced and directed by Room 214. It's a propaganda film about Beings from the NetherWorld that steal people's souls and ruin their lives. It's really quite compelling, if you close your eyes to the sex and violence. We don't have to see it if you don't want to."

"That's okay by me, Dolores. I don't need to see it. We can go for a ride in my Mercedes."

"Doesn't this car belong to Janis?"

"Er, yes it does, but it's mine for this evening. I'm glad you told me about the sex and violence. I don't like to watch sex in a movie."

Thomas is attracted to Dolores, but has to be careful how he approaches her. He doesn't want to come on too strong and scare her off.

"Dolores, do your physical troubles prevent you from.....from going out with people? I mean, do you ever invite anyone over to your Room, or go to their Rooms?"

"Yes."

"Would you like to drive over to *my* Room? I bought a new Frank Sinatra CD."

"Thomas, I'll bet you are thinking about sex."

"I am."

"So am I."

"You are?" Thomas says in great anticipation.

"Yes, I think I'll call Karen right after our date. I only like girls."

"So do I." Thomas recovers without showing his disappointment. "That's something we have in common."

It takes Thomas two weeks of hard work to convince Dolores that she can lead a normal life in the EtherWorld. She is removed from Room HYPO and reassigned to Room L, The Library. She has a great memory for technical journals. Rose is happy with Thomas and gives him yet another non-sexual hug.

★

For two glorious months, Beings in the EtherWorld have been influencing people for the Good on Earth. They even made a game of it called the Do-Good Game. As we have seen, groups of one hundred Enlightened Beings combine their energies into a powerful beam that targets a specific Human who is in need of changing his or her negative behavior. Each group has its own name and its own code word to harness the energy. The goal of the Do-Good Game is simply to influence the greatest number of Humans in a period of sixty micro-clocks. The competition is fierce, with each group trying to do do, what they do, and out do, what the other group does so well, in the Do-Good Game.

Although Thomas is not yet an Enlightened Being, his skill at pinpointing coordinates is very helpful to all the groups. He is constantly gliding and hovering in the Stratosphere, listening to and directing energy beams. He is aware that Cindy has relocated to Tampa and decides to listen in to either her wireless computer or her cellphone. He learns that she is still using dial-up, so he can't read her e-mail. He can receive Piranha's EtherNet signal, however.

Cindy e-mailed her mother a copy of the new contract she signed with Beetlesmann, his old publisher. She got a million-dollar advance. He notices that the date of the contract, and the original e-mail, was over four months old. He wonders what has been going on since, so he accesses Earth radio and satellite TV stations for news. As he progresses toward Enlightenment, he can do many things at the same time. He is able to scan and record ten sources at once. When he first came to the EtherWorld, he could scan and listen to only one.

He learns that Cindy has been working with a ghostwriter named Nerf Seedy. Mister Seedy is a competent journalist who knows the language, but who lacks imagination. He reminds Thomas of himself.

Cindy is talking to Piranha on her cellphone. There is a squeaking noise in the background. "Hello, baby, is Nerf still there?"

"Yes he is, but he's very busy," Cindy says in a strained voice.

"That's nice, honey."

I guess it's business as usual for the bitch, Thomas thinks as he continues to scan for news. *Same moldy old whore.*

He finds a news show from South Florida. It's a special program called "An Evening With the Author." Tonight's guest is Cindy Buchetta. The moderator is Calvin Quire.

"Welcome Cindy, and congratulations. Your new book, *From Pole to Pole*, has been on top of *The New York Times* best-seller list for two months. It has already sold more copies than your late husband's book, *The Princess and the Pauper*. We hear from our Quiring Reporter that it's going to be made into a movie. Any truth to that?"

"Well, Calvin, my husband's book was a movie. Since my book has outsold his, I should say 'ours,' because I really wrote most of it, doesn't it make sense that my book should also be made into a movie? It will make a better movie."

"You are a busy woman. You have the most popular nightclub in Florida, an adoring public, and a very bright future. What's next for Cindy?"

"I will tell you something, Calvin. As you know, it takes ambition, talent, good luck, and perseverance to accomplish anything. I desire to help my fellow Floridians. I have the means to do so. That's why I'm running for Governor in the next election. I'm running as a Republican, since I have befriended so many businessmen in my pole club. I call them *pole caps*, short for capitalists. Isn't that cute?"

"Er, Cindy, *pole caps* is awfully close to *polecat*, which is another name for skunk."

"It is? Well, I wouldn't want to offend anybody. You know that, Calvin."

"Yes I do, but think of the poor skunks."

Thomas glides in loop-de-loops, faster than he ever has, propelled by total and complete rage. His negative energy is so strong that it is picked up by Room 214. They dispatch Rose to the place in the Stratosphere where Thomas is listening to the TV show.

He brings Rose up to date on all the facts but doesn't tell her about Cindy's new book. She's able to piece that together herself from the signals stored in his EtherKnob receiver.

"So, it seems that Cindy has a successful book. It appears that it is even outselling your blockbuster best seller. This must be quite some book."

"Not really, it's cheap pulp trash that appeals to whores like her, who want to get rich at other people's expense."

"Thomas, you haven't read the book, have you?"

"No, and I don't want to."

"All the critics say it's very much like your work. It seems she learned well. I see cellphone conversations stored on the fourth EtherKnob wave band. She had a ghostwriter named Nerf Seedy do the writing, but she gave him the ideas.

"Thomas, tell me the truth. Did Cindy actually dictate the outline, plot, and story ideas for your books?"

"Hell no, I did the first two by myself."

"But they bombed. What about the third book, the one that went blockbuster. Did she help you with that?"

"I don't want to talk about it."

"You *have* to talk about it, or I'm going to be really pissed."

"Yeah, yeah, so she gave me a few ideas."

"A few ideas? It would seem to me that it must have been more than a few ideas. Her book has gone nutso viral. The ghostwriter is a competent wordsmith, but the meat of that book had to come from Cindy."

"It's meat all right. Raw meat."

"Now I know why you hate her so much. She was good for a lot more than washing the car. But you trusted her and you went to work at Home Depot and Walmart when a decent job wasn't available. She betrayed you in your own bed with your next-door neighbor. The sound of the box springs distracted you, so you smashed into the cement truck and wound up here. She is taking all the credit for *The Princess and the Pauper* and has been on Easy Street ever since. I hear the same squeaky sound in the cellphone conversation you recorded. Wow, she *is* a bitch.

"Okay Thomas, here is your next assignment."

"Don't even think it, Rose!"

"You have to, Thomas."

"I won't do it!"

"It's the only way you can achieve Universal Awareness. You have to love those who have injured you. Of course, you can slap them around a little bit first to make yourself feel better."

"No."

"Yes Thomas, it has been decided. You will make contact with Group 19, the one hundred Enlightened Beings closest to your Room MR, and program Cindy's coordinates into your EtherKnob transmitter. You will write the message and prepare it to be sent into her brain. Only you and I will know its contents. This has to be your private battle. Your job is to turn Cindy from Evil to Good, to put positive thoughts in her head."

"I'm not going to do it."

12

"*T*homas, have you ever wondered why you haven't seen any children? There are many up here."

"Now that you mention it, I *haven't* seen any."

"That's because you can't, not until you reach the level of Enlightenment.

"Thomas, were you an only child?"

"You know I wasn't, because you know everything. I had a brother who was eight years younger than I, but he died in a bicycle accident when I was sixteen."

"When you attain Enlightenment, you can see your brother. What was his name? "

"You know that, too. It was Seymour Regis Phineas Buchetta."

"Why are you so hostile? Jerk Being! Jerk Being! Tell me his name, and stop acting like a New York punk."

"Carlo. He was named after my grandfather, and I was named after my father. He's really here?"

"Yes, and he's Enlightened. There are no children in the NetherWorld, you know. Here, every child has the chance to grow. Even infants who perished in all manner of tragedies are now productive members of the EtherWorld. There are several dozen on Room 214 staff. I know one of them. She was only four when she died. But she matured here, and she learned what she needed here. You think I'm saucy, bossy, and sexy. I am all those things, but she *chose* who she wanted to be. She learned from her Guides and Mentors. She even learned how to grow her body, and matured to the exact age she wanted to be. She chose the same age that I was when I died, twenty-three. We will both be forever twenty-three. You should see the figure they gave her."

"Mentors? There are Mentors here? I was a Mentor to a wonderful elementary-school boy in Vermont. What kind of figure does she have? Does she have a nice....?"

"Sorry, Thomas, wrong train of thought. I should know better. Mentors are one of the greatest and most wonderful parts of the EtherWorld. When you reach Enlightenment, you will become a Guide, and you will have Mentors to further guide you in all manner of things. You will then become a Mentor to other Guides. This will go on for all Eternity. Sounds pretty good, doesn't it? Now, are you going to contact Cindy or aren't you?"

"I'll think about it."

Thomas is unable to process all the news Rose has given him. He needs to visit Room Total Peace, and his request is immediately granted. It is such a comfort to him. The Aurora Panorama is always there. The soothing sounds are always there, but they are ever-changing in subtle ways. He frees his mind and remembers an incident early in his marriage to Cindy. He was obnoxious and yelled at her because she accidentally gouged the top of his guitar with the vacuum cleaner. She screamed back at him and told him to stop acting like a New York punk. That's the same thing that Rose said to him. Cindy never vacuumed again, and it was his fault. He knows he never really evolved completely out of that adolescent behavior. He is so pleased to have the knowledge there will be a group of Mentors to help him for Eternity. He will have to abandon the punk if he is to reach Enlightenment. Thomas decides to contact Cindy.

The Earth's Stratosphere is especially beautiful on this December afternoon above Tampa. Thomas did a capacitor repair job on his EtherKnob receiver, and he is ready to capture any kind of broadcast. He already knows the brainwave coordinates and has them locked into the EtherKnob memory. When he did the repairs, he must have soldered a wire to the wrong lead. His LED display shows four brains are being monitored: Cindy, Nerf Seedy, Piranha, and a pizza delivery person. Instead of getting four separate feeds and recordings, he's getting only one. It seems their thoughts are combining in the EtherKnob. He is trying to use the crystal filter to separate them.

"Hey, baby, let's take off our clothes and do one large and one small with pepperoni and onions. Did you see what they did on Dancing with a basket of chicken wings and garlic bread last night? Time to go to bed, Cindy, my sweet oregano. Hello ma'am, that will be $27.75. Nerf, I didn't know you ordered the food. How sweet, I think I just farted. I always wanted a, keep the change. Piranha is as hot as her daughter, I know I can get her alone on their yacht. Keep the change, and she hands me twenty-eight dollars. I drive five miles for a twenty-five-cent tip. I wonder what my daughter and pepperoni do all day long."

The pizza delivery man leaves, and his brainwaves fade from Thomas's scan. Piranha is trying to decide whether she will find a boy toy on Apollo Beach or stay and make trouble between Cindy and Nerf. Thomas sends her a message to go to the beach, and he disconnects her brain monitor. He sends a message to Cindy.

I really should be alone this afternoon. This guy is beginning to crowd me, and I need some space.

"Nerf, I have to do some financial stuff this afternoon and evening. You are wonderful, but can we make it tomorrow?"

"Sure, baby, I'll see you tomorrow night." Nerf leaves and drives to Piranha's private beach house, which Cindy bought for her last week. But she isn't at home.

Thomas now has Cindy isolated without distractions. He sends her the following message.

I guess I really am a Bitch. I didn't appreciate Thomas, who was really ten times better than I am. He deserved better treatment from me. If I should get a dreaded disease, it would serve me right.

"Thomas! Rose was monitoring him. You are supposed to inject *positive* thoughts."

"I'm *positive* that she is a rotten bitch, and she will pay."

"You have been relieved of your duty to influence Cindy, and it will be undertaken by someone who doesn't have a personal agenda. You have much work ahead before you can reach Universal Awareness."

Thomas is ashamed, but seems unable to control himself when he is anywhere near Cindy or Piranha.

★

Beelzie calls the Generals to order in the banquet hall. The atmosphere is jovial, because whenever there's good news, a special meal is always on the long table. Tonight, the featured appetizer is a captured and poached Archangel. This will be followed by a main course of leg of leg, and a dessert of chocolate moose (a deep-fried moose, covered with confectioners' sugar, and dipped in a rancid tar-like substance that looks like chocolate). Beelzie asks for everyone's attention.

"Yesterday our cracked team of experts successfully completed a test intervention on a Human subject. At random, we chose the wife of a businessman in Paris, France. We pinpointed the exact coordinates with our NetherTransmitter to the precise center of her brain. We told her that her husband was cheating on her with their maid, and gave her the message that she should push him off the balcony. They live in an apartment on the thirteenth floor. Can youse guys guess what happened?"

"What? What? What?" The Generals pound the table with their fists, and they drool copiously, with bits of leg of leg sticking to their chins. "Tell us! Tell us! Tell us!"

"Kersplat," Beelzie says. "The husband is now sidewalk jam. Thirteen is our lucky number. We're in business, boys. Our scanners picked up wimp Thomas above Tampa sending a message to his widow. She's a great candidate for the NetherWorld, but the goody-brigade is trying to turn her. It's our job to make sure she remains on our path. As a matter of fact, we intend to make her much worse. Of course, the EtherWorld will attempt to counter our influence. We can't intercept their thought beams, and they can't intercept ours. Let the battle begin!"

The Generals shout, "All hail, Beelzie!" and slam their tankards down on the hard table at the same exact split second, except, again, for one general, who is one-tenth of a beat late. He will be deep-fried in yak fat for tomorrow's meal.

Cindy and Piranha's new club, The Princess and the Pauper, has been in operation for two months. She has a waiting lounge because so many people want to dine there and watch the pole dancing. Not only is the lounge full, but the customers are lined up outside the door. On some nights the wait is over two hours before you are seated. The Apollo Beach Fire Marshal posted strict occupancy rules for the club. At no time can it hold more than 300 people. They monitor all nightclubs with spot checks to ensure that the rules are followed. They don't want a fire to break out in an overcrowded club; there have been many deaths around the world from nightclub fires. Beelzie's cracked team sends Cindy a message.

It's not right for all these people to stand outside. Screw the Fire Marshal. I'll let them all come in and stand at the bar. I love a crowded room. They will be six or seven deep. More money for me.

★

Back in Room MR, the Security team picks up Beelzie the Bub's transmission. Thomas is able to isolate the signal and instantly knows it was beamed at Cindy. He doesn't know what the thought was; all he knows is that it originated in the NetherWorld. "JOY! JOY! JOY!" Thomas shouts to rouse every Being. He calls Jake with the information, and Jake orders an emergency meeting of all Room 214 staff members and the Security team. Thomas puts on his polarized sunglasses. Jake speaks.

167

"Beelzie is at it again, same old, same old. The battle between Good and Evil rages on. In some ways it does get a bit boring, because it's so predictable. I knew it was just a matter of time before they figured out how to communicate directly with the Human mind. Thomas, you have but one job, and you had better do it right. When *I* say you had better do it right, you had better listen. The punishment Beelzie would lay on you is but a little love tap compared to what I'm going to do if you screw this up. Is that clear?"

Thomas sits in his chair quivering. "Yes, Sir."

"If you send one more negative message of any kind to any Human, I'll see that you become Hun's special pet. You will be his personal manservant. You got it?"

Thomas sits in his chair quivering. "Yes, Sir."

"You are to find a way to decipher Beelzie's thought transmissions. I know we can't intercept them, but if we know what they are, we can put counter-thoughts into the Human mind. It will be much more direct and effective than a generic Good thought. Here's the straight skinny. So far, neither we nor they have the ability to block a thought transmission, but I have an idea.

"Thomas, you actually have *two* jobs. The first I just mentioned: to decipher the contents of Beelzie's messages. The second is to find a way to block his messages once ours have entered the Human mind. They did it to us with the Con Ed computer. We can't control who gets there first, but we want to be the ones who shut the other guy out. Is that clear?"

Thomas sits in his chair quivering. "Yes, Sir."

A second transmission is sent by Beelzie to Cindy. Thomas tunes his NetherKnob receiver to the finest narrow crystal setting. He uses the pass-band tuning and notch filter to isolate it. He activates the noise blanker to remove static electricity crashes from thunderstorms. Suddenly, there it is, in perfect copy. The universal translator is always activated since, although Thomas speaks English, very few others in Security do. This is the content of Beelzie's message.

Publicity is everything. The media rules. The more outrageous my behavior, the more attention I will get. Now that the bar is packed over capacity, I'm going to stand on top of it, kick over the customer's drinks, and do a striptease. I know the drinks are flammable, but it really doesn't matter.

Jake has a counter-message prepared immediately.

I must not expose myself in front of total strangers. It would be very wrong.

Cindy pushes that thought away, and begins to climb a barstool to dance on top of the bar.

"It's not working," Rose informs Jake. "She isn't listening. All those drinks she is going to spill will cause a fire. Get Thomas to send the message."

Thomas stands in position to receive the energy from the one hundred Enlightened Beings in Group 19. He sends the message.

I'd better not do that after all. Look at all the women here. The wives and girlfriends will really be pissed if I take off all my clothes, because I'm so beautiful. They won't let their men take them here anymore. I will lose money.

Cindy steps down from the barstool and refastens the first two buttons on her blouse.

Jake is upset at Thomas's message, because it isn't a positive affirmation of life. However, he does admit that it worked.

Thomas sends another message to Cindy.

I think I'll go home early tonight and let my staff run the place. Excitement and fun are great, but I'm tired and need a good rest. I don't want any trouble with the Fire Marshal, so I'll order my staff to let the crowd thin out.

Jake tells Thomas he is off the hotseat for now, but he doesn't praise his work.

Beelzie doesn't know what message Thomas sent, but he does know there was a transmission. He sends another from NetherWorld.

I think I will let my pole dancers perform nude. I know it's a violation of the Apollo Beach decency codes, but I want this club to be famous.

An interesting thing happens: Cindy self-corrects. She remembers Thomas's earlier message and dismisses Beelzie's thought.

No, I'd better not. The city might close the club, and I would lose money.

The battle continues. Thomas, and Beelzie's cracked team, know that Cindy is alone at home and that Piranha and Nerf are alone in Piranha's beach house. They prepare to intervene.

Beelzie sends a message to Cindy.

I'll bet the old lady is screwing Nerf. How could she do that to her own daughter? I'll get even with her tomorrow when the three of us go swimming. She is going to have a leg cramp, and I'll drown Nerf in the surf.

Thomas has an idea, and doesn't try to counter Beelzie's message. Instead, he sends one to Piranha.

Do I really want to lose this gravy train? Cindy is making a fortune and sharing it with me. If I screw Nerf and she finds out, I could lose everything. I'd better get rid of him. I'll bet I can send him packing.

"Nerf dear, you failed the test," Piranha says. "I was wondering whether you would be true to Cindy or chase after me. The truth is, dear, that we don't know where you've been. You could be unhealthy. I must inform my daughter. We can't be too careful. So, bye."

She immediately calls Cindy to tell her that Nerf tried to put the make on her. "I threw him out. Can you imagine the nerve! You can get another ghostwriter. Get some nice female graduate student with buck teeth."

"Thanks, Ma. He's history."

★

It isn't long before the NetherWorld cancels out the great work the Etherworld Groups had accomplished. After months of positive transmissions, now it's back to the same devolution that has been taking place for millennia. It seems that Beelzie is getting the upper hand, especially in America. The very rich and their immoral puppet lawmakers have taken all the resources from the people. Beelzie is very clever. He knows that he will eventually get most of the rich. It's the borderline Humans he's after. He wants to claim those who are still doing Good deeds.

The NetherWorld team invents a powerful new weapon. It's a rapid-fire, scattershot beam. One transmission can be beamed into as many as 500 different Human brains at the same time. His copywriters have penned some marvelous catchphrases that call the Humans to Evil behavior. He knows that other Americans will respond in kind, because they are basically sheeple. He is confident that the whole society will ultimately be dragged down. They will devolve closer and closer toward the gray line that prepares them for entry into the NetherWorld.

Beelzie sends his scattershot messages.

We need to have these wars to protect Democracy. Our security depends on being able to torture our enemies.

Social Security is bankrupt. We need to slash benefits to every retiree. We can't raise the cap on the super-rich, because it will hurt our economy.

Clean air and water rules aren't as important as American industry providing jobs. We should loosen the standards so these companies can prosper.

Freedom of speech is more important than trying to put restrictions on pornographic shows that are aimed at children.

Imported foods and drugs don't need government monitoring. People in other countries have a right to make a living.

I honestly feel that the largest percentage of our gross national product has got to be spent on new fighter aircraft and military hardware. Most Americans should be employed in defense.

Corporations are people. I believe they should be endowed with the same rights and privileges as any American citizen.

I will pay more attention to what Lindsay Lohan and the Kardashians are doing than I will to anything else.

If my neighbor is in trouble, I will not help him. He wouldn't help me if I got in trouble.

I need to buy the biggest SUV I can find. Air pollution and using too much fuel aren't as important as my neighborhood status and my safety.

It doesn't matter if I lie and cheat on my taxes, or lie and cheat to get ahead at work. The meek will inherit nothing but the hind tit.

Everybody else is doing it. Why should I be left behind?

What's wrong with steroids?

What's wrong with meth?

I don't need a spiritual life. All the Christers want is my money.

Beelzie has been quite successful in the last fifty years. He has undone much Good that Franklin Delano Roosevelt accomplished with his New Deal. He has weakened the spirit of a proud, vigorous people who won World War II, and replaced them with a generation of overweight, greedy sheeple who are drifting closer and closer to the NetherWorld.

Jake and company must circle the wagons.

13

Thomas drifts alone outside of Room MR, musing about his life in the AfterWorld. He is unsure whether he can ever purge his bad memories. Rose glides next to him.

"Hello, Thomas. You seem to be at peace."

"Yes, I need a piece."

"There's no *a* in front of the word. It's just *peace*."

"Okay, I need piece."

"Thomas, how are you spelling peace?"

"A·w·o·m·a·n·w·h·o·p·u·t·s·o·u·t."

Rose chortles with laughter. She is laughing so hard that she startles Thomas.

"What do you know? I finally heard you laugh. As a matter of fact, that's the first time I've ever seen you even smile."

"Jerk Beings can be amusing at times."

"Thanks for the compliment," Thomas says sarcastically.

"That wasn't a compliment. I'll give you the correct spelling: it's p·e·a·c·e. Now, to continue your pursuit of Universal Awareness, please glide with me."

Rose takes Thomas to a Room between Sectors A and B.

"Thomas, this is Room F, Room Fantasy. Please come inside."

Room F is semicircular. In the middle of the straight side is a very comfortable, cushioned couch. Next to the couch, on either side, are end tables with Jameson Whiskey, top-quality single-malt Scotch, and munchies of all kinds. In the half-circle part of the room are doors numbered one through twenty. They are placed with exact spacing between them. Thomas and Rose sit on the couch.

"A large part of your Universal Awareness training is to be able to see the big picture. You are a writer. You know that most fiction writers start by writing about their own experiences. Their characters are but thinly veiled versions of themselves. As they perfect their craft, they are able to create believable characters who have different personalities. It's the same with Awareness. The first is of yourself and your concerns. In order to give and receive Love, you must be able to see the big picture. This room is designed to broaden your horizons.

"The motto of Room F is, 'If you can think it, you can be it.' You will remember all those things you wanted to do, all those people you wanted to be like, and construct fantasies of any kind. When you think of one, you assign it to a door. You will remain here until all twenty fantasy doors are occupied. This is your own private room that no other Being has access to, except for me, of course."

"Of course."

"Let's say, for example, you had a fantasy about being a country doctor who saves an accident victim's life, and you assign the fantasy to door number seven. Every time you open that door, you can relive it. You can modify, change, fine tune, do whatever you like to each fantasy. If you get tired of any one, you can delete it and start over.

"There is one area that is out of bounds. You cannot have any sexual fantasies about people you know. Your fantasy interactions must be impersonal, and involve only hypothetical events as they *could* have happened. I've done this many times, and believe me, it's just like the real thing. When you walk through one of those doors, it's as if it were happening on Earth."

"What were your fantasies, Rose?"

"As I said, Thomas, this is personal, and I'm supposed to keep a professional detachment. But I can tell you one of them. I had a fantasy, which I put behind door number sixteen, that I was in the Miss Universe Pageant. I wore a tight, white satin gown with black pearls around my neck, and black stiletto heels. I put a dab of Norell perfume behind each ear and between my breasts. I didn't have on any underwear, because I didn't want the lines to show. I walked slowly down the red carpet and wiggled ever so slightly from side to side as I looked over my left shoulder."

"Rose, you aren't an Enlightened Being, you are a sadist!"

"Incentive, Thomas, incentive. You need an incentive. Now get busy and fill up those twenty fantasy doors."

It takes several clocks before Thomas can compose himself. He remembers baseball. He loved the Boston Red Sox and hated the New York Yankees. He wasn't very big or heavy. At five-foot-ten and 160 pounds, he would have played shortstop, as he did in high school.

It's the American League playoffs at Fenway Park in Boston, Massachusetts, U.S.A. The games are tied, three apiece. This is the final game.

"Don Orsillo and Jerry Remy here, and do we have us a game. It's the bottom of the ninth, and Mariano Rivera is set to deliver. The score is Yankees six and Red Sox five. Rivera has his heat working this evening, and he struck out the first two batters. Youkilis is up. Rivera gets the sign. He delivers. Whoa, a chest-high fastball brushed Kevin back."

"No, wait! You're right Jerry, it did hit him. It must have just gotten a piece of his jersey. Tony Randazzo, the home plate ump, pointed to first base. The tying run is on. Now batting for the Sox is Thomas Buchetta."

Thomas is at the plate. He usually uses a thick-handled bat and chokes up two inches. He's a spray hitter with little power, but an excellent singles guy. The designated hitter is due up next, but he's gone 0 for 4 today. Thomas decides to grab a different bat. He uses Crawford's bat, a nice, fat, caveman club. Thomas remembers Bucky Dent's shot that won the pennant for the Yanks. Dent was a shortstop who didn't have much power, like himself. Thomas knows that Rivera doesn't want a repeat, so he's not going to pitch him inside. If he got a fastball up, even a light hitter like Thomas could loft one over the Green Monster, a mere 310 feet down the line.

The right-field corner is only 302 feet, but it falls away sharply to 380 feet. If he can time Rivera, shift his left foot toward first base as he swings, he might be able to take him down the right-field line. Thomas guesses wrong. The first pitch is way inside.

"Hey, ump, he needs a warning! He already nailed Kevin," Thomas says as he turns around to look at Randazzo.

The ump scowls back at him and barks, "Play ball!"

"Jerry, you know I'm thinking about it," Don Orsillo says. "You're thinking about it. Everyone at Fenway Park is thinking about it. If Dent could do it, why not Buchetta? Here's the pitch, ball two. Buchetta adjusts his cap, spits, and steps in. Rivera delivers, here's a swing and a foul headed into the seats behind first base. Youkilis leads off first, but he won't be running here, not with two out. Rivera throws over to first to keep him close. Here's the pitch. A swing and a miss. Another 93-mile-an-hour cut fastball, Don. He's got great movement on it. The count is two balls and two strikes on Buchetta. Here's the pitch. Oh, that was close, just outside, three and two."

Thomas steps out of the batter's box, tugs his cap, touches his belt buckle, adjusts his wristbands, touches his forehead, kicks mud out of his cleats, and spits. He can barely hear the vendors in the stands, "Hot dawg heah, hot dawg!" He steps into the batter's box.

"Rivera doesn't want to walk the tying run to second base, so look for a strike here, Don. Here's the pitch, a fastball right down the middle, fouled straight back. That was his pitch, but he got under it. Rivera shakes off Posada, who sets up outside. Here's the pitch, it's a line drive headed for the right-field corner, and it's...................it's outta here! It's outta here! Buchetta took Rivera the opposite way. The Red Sox win the Pennant! The Red Sox win the Pennant!"

Thomas is mobbed by his teammates and carried off the field. He closes door number one and puts the fantasy in his memory.

He has programmed the first six doors and is ready for number seven. He takes a break to have a few shots of Jameson. Actually, a few shots turns into nearly half the bottle. He enjoys being impaired. Rose says that no Enlightened Beings ever lose control of themselves. Tonight, he's glad he isn't Enlightened, but his judgment is definitely questionable.

For number seven, he returns to Burlington High School. He wasn't very popular, even though he was on the baseball team and edited the school paper. Mostly, he was quiet, and didn't socialize much. He had a huge crush on Kim Richelieu.

Third period is about to begin. It's his senior English class, and Thomas always sits in the back of the room so he can study the girls as they come in. Kim sits right in front of him, and she usually flirts and teases him. They have gone out twice, but her parents are very strict. He had to bring her home by ten, or else. The teacher, Miss Pringleton, walks in and closes the door. Kim Richelieu is not sitting in the seat in front of Thomas. In her place is Rose. She turns around.

"Thomas, you can't have sexual fantasies about people you once knew, and lay off the Jameson." Rose disappears from the English class.

Holy Spumoni! She even edits my fantasies. A guy can't get any privacy.

He programs nineteen unique fantasies behind the doors. He is a starting guard for the Boston Celtics and wins the playoff game against the New York Knicks. He is a star Olympic athlete and wins the high jump, the long jump, and the one-hundred-meter dash. He becomes the richest man in America and buys a red Ferrari Enzo. He drives the car 225 miles an hour. He's an ace combat pilot who shoots down 25 MIGS.

Door number twenty is the last one. He's at Yankee Stadium in New York. He isn't there to play baseball. His band, Tom Buchetta and the DirtBags, has had five number one hits in a row. Their album tops all the charts. They are now as popular as all the greats were in their day: Sinatra, Presley, The Beatles, The Stones. Now it's Tom Buchetta and the DirtBags. Fifty thousand girls shriek and some try to climb on the stage. They take off their panties and throw them at the band. He finds it hard to play with all the lingerie littering the stage. A line of police is spread out right before the footlights to keep the girls from swarming.

The band has two huge cages of speakers on either side, each with fifty-megawatt arrays. They are so loud you can hear them all the way to Brooklyn. Thomas writes all the DirtBag's songs and does the arrangements. He is wearing tight black leather pants. His silk shirt is open to the waist, and he has heavy gold chains around his neck. His left ear is pierced, both in the lobe and twice in the upper part. He has five tattoos of naked women on various parts of himself.

Thomas plans to outfox Rose by having sex with a generic groupie who visits his dressing room after the performance. Since he doesn't know her name, he won't be violating the rule that Rose insisted upon. He throws a passkey to a foxy girl who is sitting in front. She drops it and about a dozen girls fight over the key. He doesn't know who will finally end up with it, and doesn't much care. He dries off, cleans himself up, and changes into his favorite jeans. He turns off all the lights except for one dim light in the corner. He hears a knock on the door.

Guess who's there when he opens it?

"Hello, Thomas. Close door number twenty, and let's go sit on the couch. I'm going to review your fantasies."

"Review? I thought you said they were private."

"They are. No one in EtherWorld knows of them except Jake, some members of Room 214, and me. Remember what I said: This is part of your Universal Awareness training. Let me see what we have here. Nope, no good. Do them over."

"What do you mean do them over? All of them?"

"No, you don't have to do all of them, but pick any three for now. Choose your least favorite three, and change the fantasies to others that are completely different."

"Change them to what?"

"That's up to you."

Thomas discards the high-school English class, the Olympic star, and the combat jet pilot fantasies. He replaces them with a great inventor who creates a new battery that will power a car for three straight years without a recharge, a long-shot candidate who becomes President of the United States, and, in door number five, he conjures up a research scientist who discovers a cure for AIDS, saving millions of lives.

"That's much better, Thomas. I'm especially glad you got rid of that jet pilot. More like door number five. Throw out the presidential candidate and the inventor, and replace them with fantasies like number five. Well done."

Thomas successfully redoes eight of his fantasies to reflect positive messages and caring for his fellow Beings. Most candidates for Universal Awareness wind up with ten or twelve, but for him, eight was extremely difficult.

★

Today, Thomas has orientation for the new employees he hired for Ristoranti Buchetta. He has four chefs: two women and their mothers-in-law. They are all from the same town and, as a matter of fact, from the same extended family. They have been in the EtherWorld for seventy-five years, so they weren't spoiled by frozen foods and TV dinners on Earth. Everything they make is fresh, from scratch.

Boots is waiting for Thomas in the restaurant. He meows nonstop for attention and is glad to see his friend. He jumps on Thomas's new lace tablecloth, tears a hole in it, and knocks over the flower vase. Thomas doesn't say "Bad kitty," because he knows Boots is testing him.

Rose glides quickly to Thomas. She is all excited.

"Thomas! Thomas! Guess who wants to come and eat at Ristoranti Buchetta?"

"Who?"

"The Number Three man in Room 214. He's Jake's assistant, and he is also the most important literary figure in history."

"Who is he?"

"The Holy Ghostwriter."

"The Holy Ghostwriter wants to eat in my restaurant? Wow! Why did he pick mine?"

"His full name is Holy Rollino. His friends call him Holy Roly, and he used to hang out in Vatican City a lot. He really misses good Italian food.

"There's only one other Italian Restaurant in the AfterWorld, but it's across the border in Sector T. It's run by Al and Lucky, Al Capone and Lucky Luciano. It's called La Casa Nostra. It's a rough place, but the food is fantastic. Beings from the EtherWorld who were just about to become Enlightened would sneak across the border and eat there. They would fill their mouths with cotton so they sounded like Marlon Brando. They would paint fake scars on their faces and wear sharkskin suits with black ties. Before Jake clamped down, it was almost an initiation rite for males who were to be Enlightened. They would sneak across, drink too much Chianti, and bring back empty .38 caliber shell casings as souvenirs. Those now command high prices on EtherBay. Beelzie was upset when they stopped coming, because Al and Lucky lost a lot of business.

"The Holy Ghostwriter and his entourage will be here on Sunday afternoon. Best to prepare now. Don't forget, your first week's receipts have to pay for that gate you damaged at the border crossing."

When Sunday afternoon arrives, so do Holy Rollino and his entourage. Rose and Thomas and the entire restaurant staff are outside to view the spectacle. There is a procession, just like in the opera *Aida*, except this one is several miles long.

Thomas says to Rose, "Look at this, they are all white, and they have wings. Even the horses have wings. They actually have golden halos and the angels on horseback are playing golden trumpets. The carriages are made of gold and have fringed canopies. There's music by the Norman Nabertwackle Choir." Thomas is all excited.

"No, Thomas. That's the Mormon Tabernacle Choir."

"Who writes this stuff? Wait, don't tell me. The Holy Ghostwriter."

Thomas seats his Holy Rolyness and tells him about the special meal he has prepared.

"Your Royal Holy Rolyness, for an appetizer I suggest Holy Moley that has been Holy Smoked. For the main dish I suggest Holy Cow that has been specially prepared by Phil Rizutto. For dessert, I suggest Holy Spumoni. In the basket are Bagels and Swiss Cheese with Holes."

The Holy Ghostwriter's trusted assistant shakes her head no, and tells Thomas to bring a large pizza with ground beef, onion, and garlic. And bring plenty of Chianti. She relays the rest of Holy Rollino's instructions on how the pizza should be prepared. He is to use King Arthur flour and Penzey's Italian seasoning, and water from New York City. The crust should be cooked so that when you use the pizza-cutter, it sounds like an angel walking across sun-melted snow. He should hear a light crunch. When you hold up a single slice of pizza, folded in half, the tip should not be limp, but the crust should not be burned. There should be some charring on the edges, like they do in Naples. "Capiche?"

"Oh yes, absolutely," Thomas says. "Tell his Holy Rolyness that we will cook it perfectly."

"Cook *them* perfectly. We want 400 pizzas and 200 cases of Chianti Ruffino. We also want you to give Boots a special treat on Roly's behalf because he loves cats. He suggests filet of Dover sole and French farmhouse field mouse. Capiche?"

Boots purrs loudly and rubs against Holy Rollino's leg. Thomas is surprised that the cat doesn't need eye protection to view him. He guesses that Boots is Enlightened.

The pizzas are perfectly cooked and the wine has already been brought out, with a case put on The Holy Ghostwriter's table. The honored guests are very fond of the wine and burst into song. They sing to the tune of "Bloody Mary" from *South Pacific*.

"Garlic pizza is the food I love,
clap, clap, clap, clap.
Garlic pizza is the food he loves.
Garlic pizza is the food he loves,
now ain't that too damn bad.

"The cheese is puffy as the white clouds above,
clap, clap, clap, clap.
The cheese is puffy as the white clouds above.
The cheese is puffy as the white clouds above,
now ain't that too damn bad.

"The sauce is tasty as a young girl in love,
clap, clap, clap, clap.
The sauce is tasty as a young girl in love.
The sauce is tasty as a young girl in love,
now ain't that too damn bad.

"Garlic pizza is the food I love,
clap, clap, clap, clap.
Garlic pizza is the food he loves.

Garlic pizza is the food he loves,
now ain't that too damn bad."

The guests hit a heavenly harmony on the word *bad*. Holy Rollino's voice is in especially fine form. They are having a wonderful time. Throughout the meal the Holy Mandolin Player plays and sings all his Holy Rolyness's favorite songs, "Torna a Sorrento," "O Sole Mio," "Finiculi, Finicula," "Volare," "Ave Maria," and his absolute favorite of all, "Ghostwriters in the Sky."

Thomas knows this is a meal that will be remembered by the EtherWorld for a very long time.

14

Every Being in the EtherWorld is talking about Holy Rollino's visit to Ristoranti Buchetta. Rose is proud of Thomas, and tells him he may invite her for an intimate candlelit dinner as soon as he is Enlightened. Thomas suggests they go right now to the restaurant he saw in the Andromeda Galaxy, just after he had elevated a toll-booth life form to Being status.

"Rose, you would really like this place. How about Saturday night?"

"Thomas, Room 214 frowns upon using a communal SlingShot for recreation. You need one of your own, and that's only by special decree. I am familiar with that restaurant. As you well know, Beings who eat there have sex at the same time. You had better be careful. If they served a decent jelly doughnut, I would probably prefer it to you. Nice try, Higher Life Form. Strike three."

Thomas is summoned to Room 214. There to greet him is Holy Rollino's assistant. She asks him to follow her, and tells him he doesn't need his special polarized sunglasses. She takes him into a huge auto showroom. There, sitting on a raised platform, is a glistening cobalt blue vehicle, repainted like his 1994 Ford Mustang. He is now the proud owner of the SlingShot he used for his Explorer trip. It has been freshly waxed, and the same fuzzy white dice are hanging from the rearview mirror.

The assistant hands him the keys and says, "Congratulations! His Royal Holy Rolyness, The Holy Ghostwriter, liked his pizza with ground beef, onion, and garlic so much, he wanted you to have this as a present to drive wherever you want."

Thomas gives the assistant a big, non-sexual hug (he's trying to learn), and she smiles. He raises the Mustang SlingShot's clear glass canopy and steps into the driver's seat. On the passenger's seat next to him, wrapped in white glitter-paper with a gold ribbon, is a package. He opens it and finds a tapestry-bound book, *The Holy Ghostwriter's Book of Metaphors*. Thomas opens the book and reads the Holy Table of Contents: "How to recognize a bad metaphor. How to make a bad metaphor work for you. How to recombine ridiculous objects and events into workable, surrealistic metaphors." Holy Rollino's book is the greatest ever written on the subject. Thomas is all excited, and can't wait to study it. He may finally be able to write a blockbuster best-seller.

He takes his new SlingShot back to Room MR and is an instant celebrity. He proudly shows off his book to Bill Buckley, who is visiting Joe. It seems that Roly consulted with Bill on some of the contents. Bill has a personally autographed edition of his own.

All afternoon, Thomas gives rides. Instead of gliding to see Rose outside of Room 214, he drives over. She is very impressed and a bit jealous. She doesn't have a SlingShot of her own.

"So, Rosie baby, what do you think of my new wheels?"

"Not bad, I suppose. There are many people who have done good works in the EtherWorld, and not all of them are given their own high-speed fun cars."

"Are there other privately-owned SlingShots?" Thomas asks.

"Oh sure, several hundred million, I'm certain." Rose really has no idea.

"So, do you want to go for a ride?"

"Not today, thank you, but perhaps we can use it for your next assignment. I'll tell you about that later."

After leaving Rose, Thomas sees another SlingShot running parallel to him. Instead of a clear glass canopy, it's ruby-frosted, and he can't see the Being or Beings inside. Thomas floors his Mustang, but the other SlingShot leaves him in the stardust. Thomas feels humiliated, but has an idea.

He drives to Room L, the Library, and looks up auto customizing. He specifically wants a Room for Ford racing engines. He finds one in Sector C.

Thomas's Mustang SlingShot has only the small-block 289-cubic-inch engine, putting out about 250 horsepower. He instructs the expert technicians to install the Shelby Cobra engine. It's a seven-liter, 427-cubic-inch monster that generates 425 horsepower. It would propel the Shelby Cobra at close to 170 miles per hour and acceleration was mind-boggling. Since his car weighs about 1,000 pounds less than the Cobra, he expects to top out at 225 miles per hour. This is the exact speed of the Ferrari Enzo he drove in his fantasy for door number six, in Room F.

With the engine newly installed, he pulls into a Green Brothers gas station, and fills up with the highest octane fuel available. I know you've never heard of the Green Brothers Oil Company. All the ones you are familiar with, Exxon/Mobile, British Petroleum, Shell, Amoco, Chevron/Texaco, Marathon/Speedway, and their CEOs, are in the NetherWorld as punishment for actions that ruined the Earth's environment.

With a fresh tank of pollution-free Green gas, Thomas cruises on Main Street, a four-lane highway between Sectors C and D. He is stopped at a red EtherLight, when the same ruby-frosted SlingShot pulls next to him. Both Shots rev their engines. Thomas is ready to pop the clutch. The EtherLight turns green, and they leave a patch of rubber a hundred feet long. They are nose to nose, 0 to 30, 30 to 60,

60 to 120, 120 to 225 mph. No one can pull away, and they are even as they approach the next EtherLight and have to slow down. Thomas gets the license plate number of the ruby-frosted SlingShot. He's going to check the register to see who owns it. He must get more horsepower out of that 427 Cobra engine. He intends to beat the ruby-frosted Being.

★

Thomas puts a supercharger on the Cobra engine, and now has the fastest SlingShot in the EtherWorld. Unfortunately, he receives a citation from Highway Security for too much noise. He is told to install quieter mufflers. Thomas complains that it will rob some of his engine's horsepower, and he would then not be the fastest, but they insist. When the Highway Security Patrol is absent, he opens up the baffles and races around the Galaxy.

He has the Mustang roaring loudly as he pulls up to Gabriel's Hideaway. He loves to make a grand entrance. Bill and Joe are sitting at their favorite table, and he asks if he can join them.

"Sure," Joe says. "That's a neat SlingShot you got there, kid. That's when America was America, when men were men and women were women. Now men are women, and women are men, women no longer like men and like women instead, and we got Hondas, Kias, and Toyota Corollas. Shit Corolla sounds like it should have been a cigar. Its engine sounds like four chipmunks spitting, nee nee nee nee. Where's the good old American roar from a throaty V-8? I'll tell you, Bill. The Pinkos want to ruin our economy by flooding the U.S. market with toy cars. I ask you, why would a real man ever want to drive one?"

"It seems to me that you have answered your own question. There's no obfuscation; it's perfectly logical. Since there are no real men left, there is no need for a real man's conveyance."

The Hideaway is crowded tonight, and groups of people are in lively discussions. The Jameson is flowing freely, and the patrons are boisterous. All is not gaiety, however, and an argument breaks out among the patrons sitting at the tables near the East bar.

"What do you know about being a Christian? Saint Peter founded the one true church. All you Protestants are just knockoffs. Shit, Henry the Eighth started the Church of England, and King James rewrote the Bible, so Henry could behead his wives. Martin Luther was anal retentive and was simply jealous of the Pope. He saw a great opportunity to make money, that's all."

"Pope, dope, hope, nope, get a rope. Celibacy, oh I'm sure, as long as little boys aren't around. You papists are as holy as a pack of wolves."

A Presbyterian Minister enters the fray. "Mine is the one true Church." He is answered by a Baptist Preacher from Alabama. "Ya'll are heretics and will burn in Hell."

"Mine is the true Church," says a preacher from Tennessee. "We handle serpents as we are told by the Bible to do. Praise the Lord!"

"Mine is the true Church. We have the right method, that's why we are called Methodists. You Catholics use the rhythm method. That's why there are too many of you."

"Up yours, Methodist. Birth control is ungodly."

Joining the combatants are Muslims, Jews, and the faithful of other religions who have been listening intently.

A Sunni Muslim is speaking to a Shiite Muslim. "Mine is the true religion. You do not worship Allah the right way. You are all wrong and are a blasphemer." The Shiite replies, "No. He is *our* Allah, not yours. I prove it by cutting myself with this knife, and I bleed for Allah."

"Oh yeah? I will prove I am right by cutting myself twice with my knife. I will bleed twice as much for Allah."

"Says you! I cut my self *three* times, plus I cut your head off."

The two Muslims get into a vicious knife fight and knock over the tables. The Arbitrators finally pull them apart and bring iodine, gauze bandages, and surgical tape. The bickering continues. Thomas musters up his courage, walks into the middle of the fray, and asks what they are fighting about.

A Jewish Rabbi is the first to answer. "I believe we are fighting about who has the real God. They are all crazy. Our God, Jehovah, is the oldest and the best. He is the one true God."

"You Christ killer, you don't know anything!" a Fundamentalist cleric shouts.

"You call *me* a Christ killer. You Protestants and Catholics in Northern Ireland are killing each other over the same Christ. You are all Christ killers!"

"God is not Jehovah, He is Allah!"

"God is not Jehovah or Allah, She is Minerva."

"God is Yahweh."

"You will burn in the everlasting fires of NetherWorld if each of you does not contribute twenty dollars to my television ministry!"

"The Great Spirit is God. My God is real, yours are man-made!"

"Martin Luther is nothing but a defrocked Catholic. You and your misled cronies are also-rans!"

"You are a pig-eating, unclean sybarite Infidel!"

The combatants begin throwing peanuts at each other. It escalates to ashtrays, and things are really getting ugly. Everyone is now standing on chairs and shouting at the top of their lungs, waving their arms, and verbally assaulting anyone who is within earshot.

"My name is Torquemada. I poured hot lead into people's ears for the Lord!"

"My name is Jim Jones. I poisoned 918 people with Kool-Aid for the Lord!"

"My name is Tammy Faye Bakker, and I put on my fake eyelashes for the Lord!"

"My name is William Graham, Sr. My son is so holy they named a cracker after him!"

"The one true God is Konitchencock! All your other Gods are anemic by comparison! Deep in the jungles of Borneo, our tribe has worshiped Konitchencok for five thousand years! Konitchencock has the biggest penis of all the Gods in the EtherWorld! That is how Humans were created! All babies are born because Konitchencock planted his seed! Let me hear you shout Amen! Again, let me hear you shout Amen!"

Thomas has heard enough. He places one table on top of another and stands on it. He is now the tallest person in the

Room. Balanced precariously, he surveys the scene. There's blood, broken furniture, and glass on the floor. The noise is so loud you can barely hear the person speaking right next to you. Thomas screams as loud as he can.

"Everybody shut the fuck up!" There is now silence in Gabriel's Hideaway.

Thomas lowers his voice. "I have only one thing to say. Jake is going to be really pissed when he hears that you have learned absolutely nothing since you have been in the EtherWorld. You may find yourselves at the bottom of Sector E, and some of you may even be sent across the border into Sector F, but that is not for me to judge. If I hear one more person say that his is the one true religion, I'm going to perform a circumcision on that person's head. Do I make myself clear?"

Thomas walks back to the table seating Joe and Bill. "Although your imagery was graphically overstated, I do believe you achieved your intended purpose," Bill says as he pours the three of them a full glass of Jameson.

Thomas is summoned to Room 214.

★

Today is a great day in the AfterWorld of Thomas Buchetta. Rose is smiling. She takes his hand and tells him to grab his polarized sunglasses. The two Beings glide to Room 214. Jake himself makes a rare Supreme Being-to-

Being communication. The ritual is generally delegated to the Director of Promotions, who executes Jake's Holy Orders, but this time Jake speaks directly to Thomas.

"Thomas, what you did in Gabriel's Hideaway is the high point of your life in EtherWorld. Not only did you do the right thing, but you used My Name in the best way possible. You have demonstrated wisdom that is rarely achieved by those who are not Enlightened. You are hereby promoted from Room MR in Sector D to your own Room in Sector C. You may choose your own Room name. For the first time in our history, a restaurant will reside within a Sector. You can move Ristoranti Buchetta right next to your Room, and I'll make sure you have a three-car garage for your SlingShot. You never know, you might buy another car or a boat, or have too much junk in the house and need storage space."

After five clocks, Thomas completes the move into his new Room. He decides to call it Room Renaissance instead of Room Communications. He wants to attract those who have great accomplishments in many different areas. He feels they will be the most interesting Beings to have around. There's space for thousands, and he can't wait to see who wants to move in. Rose tells him the next part of his Universal Awareness training will be to find Beings with whom he is compatible; he will be spending much time with them.

"Thomas, you have to be careful about slobs. When I was in Sector B, in the Nurses Room, I shared space with two broads who never picked up after themselves. One was Russian and the other was German. You cannot believe how annoying it was to have to endure Wagner and Shostakovich records all night long, while I cleaned sauerkraut and pierogi stains off the couch. You must be selective."

Thomas picks Rose up outside Room 214, and they set off for Room THAFNI, The Holding Area for New Initiates. She tells him to advertise his Room by placing a notice on the bulletin board. With his Ristoranti Buchetta receipts, he can also place some ads on the EtherRadio station, WJOY. Thomas asks Rose if she would like to drive his Mustang SlingShot.

"Sure, I've never driven a Mustang before. Oh my, this car *is* fast." Rose is having a great time on the EtherFreeway, en route to Room THAFNI, but she doesn't allow for the car's speed and gets too close to the stanchion guarding the toll booth. She bashes in the left front fender, and it pinches the tire so the SlingShot can't be driven. The front of Thomas's car is quite a mess. He keeps his composure and tells Rose that it wasn't her fault.

"It's only a front fender. Please don't feel bad. You would feel much better if...."

"No, I wouldn't. I'm sorry I bashed your car, but don't even say it. Here we are, 270 blinks from anywhere, and I'm not dressed in my gliding clothes. We're going to have to hitch a ride."

Thomas and Rose stand alongside the EtherFreeway and stick out their thumbs. Rose lifts her dress halfway up her thigh and smiles.

"Where did you get the idea to do that?" He is surprised.

"From a Room 214 propaganda film called *It Happened One Night*, starring Clark Gable and Claudette Colbert."

Thomas doesn't have time to ask her why it was a propaganda film, because the same ruby-frosted SlingShot he had been racing pulls up to offer them a ride.

"By all means, do get in. I'll be happy to take you wherever you want to go."

The driver is a good-looking man, about thirty-five, with a touch of silver gray at his temples. He wears a very expensive English wool suit. The dashboard of his SlingShot has every imaginable feature of the world's finest Ferraris and Lamborghinis. There is a bar in the back with expensive French champagne. Thomas sits in the rear, and Rose sits in the front passenger's seat. Rose asks the driver if he's an Enlightened Being. She can usually tell, but he is hard to read.

"Pleased to meet you. My name is Ralph Farquatt, with two Ts and one R, and yes, I'm an Enlightened Being. What is your name, darling? You sure are a pretty Being."

Ralph doesn't ask Thomas his name, and it's hatred at first sight between the two men. "My name is Thomas, so glad you asked," he says sarcastically.

"Oh yes, quite. So glad to meet you as well."

Thomas is extremely jealous and is about to lose it. He would get in big trouble for punching an Enlightened Being, but he senses something isn't quite right. He doesn't know exactly what it is.

Ralph asks Rose if she would like to listen to some music on his custom CD player, with extra-loud bass-boom module. He doesn't wait for her answer, and instead chooses rap music from Snoop Dogg.

Rose shouts the Intruder Alert Code: "INTA! INTA! INTA!" Three short micro-clocks later, Highway Security has the SlingShot surrounded by high-speed EtherPatrol cars. She grabs Thomas and pulls him out of the back seat. She talks to a Security officer.

"We have an intruder from the NetherWorld, who must have captured and modified one of our SlingShots. He is posing as an Enlightened Being to lure unsuspecting females into his vehicle. I suspect he would have tried to vaporize Thomas. He blew his cover when he played that Evil music."

"Vaporize *me*! I'll kick his Satanic ass!" Thomas attempts to get around the two patrolmen, who are slapping handcuffs on the NetherWorld Being. The ruby-frosted SlimeShot is impounded and taken to the scrap yard.

"Thomas, I admire your courage, but you are no match for an EUS Being. That's an Extreme Ultimate Slime Being. It's the highest rank you can attain in the NetherWorld, similar to an Enlightened Being here. I also like the way you were jealous back there," Rose says coyly.

What was a scary episode has suddenly turned golden. He is on EtherCloud Nine. To save them seven hours gliding time, the Security Officer drives Thomas and Rose back to Thomas's new Room.

15

*T*homas has become a frequent visitor to Room Total Peace. He often meditates for hours on one miniscule aspect of life in the AfterWorld. He used to obsess about his life on Earth, the things he did, the things he wishes he had done, and the things he wishes he had not done. Lately, it has been different. Philosophical thoughts race through his mind. He remembers reading Dante's *Divine Comedy*. The Beings in Paradiso have virtues of Prudence, Fortitude, Justice, Temperance, Faith, Hope, and Love. The Beings in the Inferno have vices of Usury, Hypocrisy, Violence, Anger, Greed, and Thievery, to name but a few.

Thomas has a difficult time understanding the relationship of the physical to the spiritual world. Humans can't have spiritual thoughts without a physical Being. Thoughts aren't pure energy, like a radio wave. Violence, for example, involves the act of destroying or hurting. It originates with a strong negative *emotion* that is acted out and made real by a physical Being. In the AfterWorld, if a Being *thinks* violent thoughts, they are still violent. However, it is the *memory* of actual physical violence that is being recollected. Without the physical act, there can be no memory.

So, it is not the act of thinking alone that produces the Good or Evil in a Being. It is the experience in real time of feeling the emotion *and* acting out the thought. When combined, they result in Evil.

Thomas wonders if the purest thoughts, and likewise the purest Goodness, are those which don't originate with physical action, but spawn themselves as the offspring of other positive thoughts. The same would be true of Evil. If Good or Evil can be abstractions, they can be self-generating, and grow in tangents and directions that don't need a physical root.

Beings in other Galaxies, who have a completely different physical makeup, will have a completely different moral code. Their base, their primary definitions, would be different. If they don't have awareness of an AfterWorld, how does that alter their behavior? As soon as Thomas's SlingShot is repaired, he intends to drive to the Vela Constellation and find out.

He has given himself a serious headache, and returns to Room Renaissance.

Thomas hears a horn beeping outside. His Mustang is parked in front of the garage. He looks into the canopy and sees Rose behind the wheel. She is revving the engine.

"Since I bashed the fender, I felt the least I could do was pick your car up from the repair shop."

Thomas checks the EtherOdometer and notices that it has logged enough miles to have gone to Sector D and back four times.

"Rose."

"Yes, Thomas?"

"Did you come straight here after you left the repair shop?"

"Of course not. I've been joyriding around EtherWorld for five clocks. Now I know how to drive it. We're going to have to work on this engine. I've been racing around with Janis, and her Mercedes is faster. She beat me by two lengths to Warp 225 MPH. We had a great time. Hope you don't mind."

"Not at all, you can borrow it any time you want."

"Good, thank you. I have a date tomorrow night for a Swirl, and I'd like to pick him up in your car."

"Strike three, Rose. Even a Jerk Being like me knows when he is being teased. Why do you do this?"

"Incentive, Thomas, incentive. I saw the request you made to visit the Constellation Vela to learn about other Sentient Beings. This is absolutely fabulous. You will exceed all requirements. Your visit counts as extra credit towards completion of Universal Awareness."

"How much longer do you think it will take me? How long do I have to work in the Enlightened Step before I complete it?"

"Thomas, perhaps I didn't explain it properly. This is really your last step. Once you reach Enlightenment, you are there. You are through. Jake feels that all the growth that happens after that is no longer part of schooling, it is optional. You may choose to stay as you will then be, or go on to advanced studies. I'll tell you more about that later. It's very complicated. I happen to have my doctorate. I would like to tag along to Vela, if you don't mind. Please don't mention that sexy-food restaurant. I know it's on the way."

"Don't flatter yourself, Rose. I was thinking about my studies, not getting you alone in the SlingShot."

"That's what your *mouth* says, but the rest of you is twitching and quivering."

"Rose, did anyone ever tell you that you're a pain?"

Thomas and Rose have a pleasant ride at Warp 225 MPH. The trip was made without his uttering any sexual innuendos. This makes Rose uncomfortable, and she wonders if she looks okay. She checks her lipstick in the passenger's sunshade mirror.

They stop at a toll booth just outside the Constellation Vela, and the same Being Thomas saw in Andromeda has been reassigned here. They say hello to Welcome Thomas, who is now aware of his existence. Thomas hands Welcome Thomas another banana, and asks Rose why the toll is one banana.

"I really have no idea if it's symbolic, or if they actually eat it. I'll have to ask Jake. When you contact another Sentient Being, I'm going to let you do all the talking. Remember, I'm just tagging along. Plus I know you have very specific ideas about what you'd like to accomplish."

"Thanks Rose, here we go."

Thomas cruises at thirty-five MPH Impulse Power above a very beautiful planet. It looks like Earth, only about three times the diameter. Like Earth, it looks like a fragile jewel in a vast sea of blackness. He docks the SlingShot in the upper atmosphere. He and Rose make contact with a Sentient Being. Rose agrees to help Thomas with translation, since she has more experience.

"My name is Thomas, and she is Rose. Mellow greetings to you from the Northern Milky Way."

"What's happening, bro?" The Being slaps his hand, and they bump fists, then one hand on top of the other, and then elbow to elbow. "'Sup Thomas? My name is Shaquille. Wait, don't tell me, you're working on your Masters, and you want to study me."

"Something like that. I want to know your philosophy. You are primarily composed of bright light and hard mineral substances. You can apparently flex any part of yourself at will, and you are about twelve feet tall by Earth standards. Your daily life has got to be different than ours. Does your belief system include an AfterWorld?"

"Say what?"

"An AfterWorld."

"After what? Thomas, I believe you're confused. You and I are both dead, bro, so we *have* to be in another World. Did you mean to ask me if I'm aware that I'm standing right here, right now? That's a bit insulting, don't you think?"

"I don't mean to be insulting. I guess I am confused."

"Follow me, guys, and I'll show you how we live on our planet. Our PR department is worth shit. Our planet doesn't have a name, only a number, HD85512b. How can anyone have fond memories of a home that's called HD85512b?

"See here, Thomas. See here, Rose. Look what that living Being is doing. He's removing the top part of his head and putting it on a designated shelf. There's a compartment with his name on it."

"Shaquille, what is that part?"

"It's his conscience. On HD85512b, we remove it first thing in the morning, so we can screw each other's mates, lie, cheat, steal, all do that good shit that we see on television. We learned from the Americans. Anyone who watches Fox news can't be bothered by the inconvenience of having a conscience. Since we perfected the removal technique, our conscience isn't aware of what's happening. According to it, we never do Evil or experience guilt. Do you dig? We pick it up at the end of the day. Only on Sunday do we leave it on all the time, like the Governor of Texas does, so others will *think* we're holy.

"Check this out. Since I know you two are Human Beings, I've programmed my speech pattern so it would be most recognizable. I tried Spanish, Italian, Swedish, Chinese, French, and all them other tongues, but I like Rap best. I've used it as my model. Everything we learn about Earth comes from your television transmissions. Our culture is based on them: *The Texas Chainsaw Massacre, Celebrity Death Match, South Park,* and my personal favorite, *The Playboy Club.* Do you know about the TV game show *Jeopardy*?"

Rose says no, but Thomas says yes. Thomas asks Shaquille what time *The Playboy Club* is broadcast. Rose pokes Thomas in the ribs so hard that he drops the *TV Guide* Shaquille just handed him. Thomas tells Rose that Shaquille's people must have seen the movie *Galaxy Quest.* The Beings in that movie also learned everything about Earth from television. He whispers to her, "Rose, that was fiction. How can this *really* be happening? Who writes this stuff?"

Shaquille continues, "I'm glad you are familiar with *Jeopardy*, Thomas. As you know, the contestant always gives his answer as if it were a question. That's the way we talk here. Everything is back asswards. If you want someone to go, you tell them to stay. If you think they are ugly, you tell them they're gorgeous. If you want to take all their money, you say you're going to give them a tax cut or some other trifle. The combination of no conscience, backwards speech, and total lack of logic, was patterned after the bylaws of the Republican National Committee in Texas, on your home Planet. We saw it on Fox News.

"Ya'll take care. If you need anything else, just ask."

★

Thomas drops Rose off at Room 214 and goes home. He doesn't feel any wiser after talking with Shaquille, but he did learn when *The Playboy Club* would be broadcast. He decides to separate the physical and spiritual for now. He isn't Enlightened enough to understand the intricacies. Since Thomas has always loved astronomy, he decides to shop for the best telescope he can buy in EtherWorld. He will learn about the physical Universe, and then try to understand its Sentient Beings and their relationship to it, especially how the Playboy Bunnies fit into the Milky Way.

Boots enters Thomas's Room through his special kitty door. Right behind him is an orange tabby. She is the same cat that Thomas petted when he was outside the Forum Restaurant.

"What's going on? Do you have a new friend? How did she glide all the way up here?"

Thomas is totally blown away because he can understand the message that Boots sends him. "We're faster than you are. Did you ever try to race a cat?"

The female cat talks to Thomas. "Hi, my name is Tabitha. Pleased to meet you. Could we have a little privacy, please?"

Boots and Tabitha disappear into a corner of Thomas's electrical lab. He'd set up a kitty condo, complete with scratching post and heated kitty bed, as Boots's special place.

Thomas wonders if cats can have virtual kittens in the EtherWorld. If he can remember children, they can remember kittens. He had no idea that cats had such power. Until now, all he's heard from Boots is meow. He could be an imposter. Perhaps he's a NetherWorld Being who's impersonating a cat. Thomas calls Rose in a panic, on his EtherPhone.

Rose is chortling again. "So, Higher Life Form, Boots and Tabitha surprised you."

"It's not fair, Rose. Even Boots gets it. Why won't you let me make love to you?"

"My dear Thomas. You must not put the chicken before the egg. What is *it*? Is *it* number.....

1 – A quick screw in the backseat of a SlingShot?

2 – Or sex with your married neighbor on his or her kitchen table?

3 – Or a different partner every week to see whose private parts feel best?

4 – Or a threesome or a fivesome on the beach, so you can spread social diseases to each other?

5 – Or is it waking up each morning with the same partner, building a life of love and trust? He puts himself all around her, and she puts herself on top of him. They wake up at one o'clock in the morning and decide to make a pizza. At dawn, they take a shower together. They go shopping in the afternoon, go for a swim, and in the evening they watch a movie. They go to bed, and do something completely different the next night.

"So, Thomas, what number would you like?"

"Number 5! Number 5! And perhaps number 1 if it's the same person as number 5. 2, 3, and 4 aren't bad, as long as the same person from number 5 is there."

"That's a creative answer, Thomas, which I didn't expect. You have the right idea. The EtherWorld is no different from Earth. We can Swirl with whomever we please. But if we form an attachment to a Special Being, that is very rare and precious. When you chase after anything and everything that could possibly be female, you don't present yourself as an endearing companion. Best to remember that."

"Rose, it's you I want," Thomas says. But Rose has hung up and doesn't hear his comment.

Thomas decides to glide over to Gabriel's Hideaway. Whenever he is unhappy or perplexed, that is one of the two places he chooses. The other is Room Total Peace.

Thomas is amazed: Gabriel's now has entertainment. A bandstand is set up right near the center fountain. Tonight the Beings in Room 27 are giving a concert, and the place is packed. Janis is singing "Take another little piece of my heart now, baby," and Thomas is doing cartwheels in delight. He races home and gets his Mark IV Selmer tenor and joins the band. For three sets they wail and sing old and new songs. Kurt Cobain asks everyone's attention. There's a little feedback on the microphone, so the bartender turns the house PA system down a notch.

"Listen, everyone. I have an announcement. Janis has just been named to the staff of Room 214. She is to be the Music Director of the entire EtherWorld. She has also been promoted to Sector B. We will miss her in Room 27, but they couldn't have picked a better Being for the job."

The entire bar erupts in applause, whistles, and table pounding with beer bottles. Lenin and the Bolsheviks clap rhythmically and shout "Da! Da! Da!"

"I have another announcement. Christopher Reeve has been named head of Security, and his wife, Dana, has been named to direct a special Mentor Program for Difficult Initiates."

Again the bar breaks out in spontaneous applause.

Thomas approaches Christopher Reeve. "Hello Chris, my name is Thomas. I'm sorry about your accident and Dana's death."

"Thomas, Thomas, thank you, but sorrow is not the emotion you should feel. Dana always wanted to serve her fellow Beings, and now she has her chance. I always wanted to be a real Superman. You know, it's neat. You've heard the introduction to the show, 'Faster than a speeding bullet, more powerful than a locomotive, able to leap tall buildings with a single bound.' On Earth, there were times I actually identified with Superman and wished I could have those powers. Here, I'm living my dream. I *am* faster than a speeding bullet. You can do what *you* dream. Start writing your blockbuster novel."

"Chris, how do you know about that?"

"I'm Enlightened. I know Rose didn't tell you this, but if you write your novel, and it is for the Good, you are absolutely guaranteed top status as an Enlightened Being. Don't forget to read Holy Rollino's book. Your metaphors need a bit of work."

★

Thomas is convinced that Enlightenment is where it's at. But no matter how hard he tries, he can't send positive vibes to Cindy or Piranha. He knows he will never achieve his goal unless he honestly changes his behavior. He asks himself why he gives her so much power. Why can't he pity her for the horrible mess she's made of her life? Why doesn't he try to contact his parents or try to leave them a message? Both their sons were taken from them. Why doesn't he give them a thought? Rose is correct, he *has* much work to do.

He decides to leave Cindy alone for a while and to concentrate on the physical Universe. Spirituality is a difficult subject for him. Talking with Shaquille proved that he must reconsider his philosophy. Not that he has yet formulated one, because there is still so much to discover. There's the debate about the Prime Mover versus the Universe always existing. It makes his head spin.

Ristoranti Buchetta is doing very well, so he has the funds to purchase the best EtherScope from Room Astronomy. It's *way* more powerful than the best electron microscope on Earth. It has a direct digital feed into the sight lobe of his mind, in stereo. He doesn't have to close one eye.

He builds a platform on top of his roof that is open to the sky. Naturally, he has walls around his room for privacy. He didn't have a roof at first, because there's no rain in the AfterWorld, but soon realized that he must add one. So many people were gliding over his house to see what he was doing, it became a real nuisance.

The EtherScope can resolve something the size of a flea, 30 light-years from Earth. To give you an idea of its power, if he were to aim it at Earth and focus on a single person, one hair on that person's arm would completely fill the screen. One cell of that hair would still be so large, you couldn't see any boundaries. A single molecule would appear approximately twenty times the size of a basketball.

It's a voyeur's dream. He sees everything that's going on in far-distant Swirls.....that is, until Rose finds out what he's doing and places parental control filters on his EtherScope. He is convinced Dr. Rose von Kolisch wants to torture him.

16

The battle for control of Human minds rages throughout the AfterWorld. Thomas is summoned to Room Security on the double. Beelzie has engaged his ScatterShot weapon successfully into many minds. The EtherWorld teams can barely keep up with him. And now it seems he has a new weapon. The Enlightened Security Specialist, Kiwi, briefs Thomas.

"The Evil computer Generals have devised a new way of disrupting our energy beams into Human minds. They are using something called AutoCorrect. When we send messages for people to do Good, key words are changed by Beelzie's new device. For example, a word like 'able' is changed to 'anus,' and a word like 'caring' is changed to 'sparring.' The Human who gets our message is really getting a twisted message from the NetherWorld. It's quite clever, and we don't know how to stop him. I know Beelzie is laughing at us. He's making too many unchecked gains, and our whole program is in trouble."

Thomas shifts his mind into overdrive. His determination is fierce, and he barks out orders at the same time as he praises the work of those around him. The Security team is functioning like a well-oiled machine (he still hasn't read

Holy Rollino's book), and they quickly find a solution. As a team, they create a manual override to Beelzie's AutoCorrect.

The two Worlds are now on an even footing, since Thomas can also decipher the NetherWorld's ScatterShot energy beam. He unashamedly copies their technology and creates a similar one to send positive messages. He betters their beam by increasing the intensity of the signal. This doubles the number of Humans who can be reached by ScatterShot.

★

Beelzie is meeting with the Generals in the banquet hall. The mood is jovial, in spite of the minor setback on their AutoCorrect jammer and the EtherWorld ScatterShot weapon.

"Listen up, youse guys, this is important. First I would like to congratulate all of youse for a job well done. Before we talk about the future, let's take a moment to look at what we've already accomplished.

"Item number one. Wisconsin Governor Scott Walker has convinced his Legislature to strip state workers of their right to collective bargaining. He made the statement that he will use the National Guard to break the public union. He is also slashing benefits for state workers. Two-thirds of the corporations in Wisconsin pay no taxes. All I can say is, well done, Scott Walker, you're our guy. Let's give him a round of applause and a tankard slam."

The Generals all respond with hearty belches and screams. This time all the tankards hit the table at the same time.

"Item number two. Michigan Governor Rick Snyder has created a panel of Emergency Managers. He wants to give them the power to break union contracts and remove lawfully elected officials. Well done, Rick Snyder.

"Item number three. New Jersey Governor Chris Christie has the do-gooders scurrying for their holes. He demands that workers pay more for pension and health benefits. The changes will be legislated, not negotiated. He will destroy collective bargaining in New Jersey.

"Item number four. Ohio Governor John Kasich has signed a law limiting bargaining by 350,000 police, teachers, firefighters, and other public workers. Way to go, John Kasish! Ohio doesn't need police or firefighters. We want to watch your society disintegrate.

"Item number five. This guy is my favorite. Maine Governor Paul LePage ordered state workers to remove a thirty-six-foot mural from the State Labor Department. It depicts the state's labor history. The mural has all this touchy-feely shit about the 1937 shoe strike in Lewiston, and posters of Rosie the Riveter at the Bath Iron Works. Here's the best part.

Francis Perkins was a real pain in the ass. She was the first woman cabinet minister in American history. She was also one of the most accomplished ministers. She and her boss, Franklin Delano Roosevelt, formed the New Deal and started Social Security. They also created unemployment insurance, the right of workers to unionize, the minimum wage, and the forty-hour work week, all this unspeakable filth. Hey youse guys, do you know what LePage did?"

"What?" The Generals shout as they pound the tables.

"LePage took Perkins's name off the conference room door. He said the conference room names were not in keeping with the department's pro-business goals. Now *there's* a beautifully placed dagger into the hearts of average working Humans."

"Dagger! Dagger!" The generals all shout in unison.

"He added the phrase 'Open for Business' to the 'Welcome to Maine' sign. Listen up, youse guys, I know a future NetherWorld General when I see one. Don't you agree?"

"General! General! General!" All shout in unison.

"We can use a PR guy like him. Listen to this. All these governors are Republicans. What does that tell us, boys? I'll tell you what that tells us. I'm telling you that Republicans are our people."

"Our people! Our people! Our people!"

"Let's stand up and give a round of applause to ourselves. You will all get Distinguished Service medals for your performances.

"Now to the future. Iowa Governor John Davis is a Republican, and he's leaning toward our position. His state has been hit hard by the Human recession, and Iowa has cut social services. He's getting input from two sides. One side wants to cut health benefits and collective bargaining rights in the NetherWorld way. The other side is telling him to increase taxes on corporations and agribusiness, and leave the workers alone. He has a special legislative session in seven clocks. It's our job to prepare persuasive messages for his puny brain. If we can succeed with Davis, we can turn the whole country. Workers will slip from the middle class into oblivion. Many won't be able to afford medical treatment and will die."

"Die! Die! Die!" The generals slam their tankards down at the same time, except for General Nuisance, who was one-tenth of a second late. Beelzie gave him a dispensation because he was in such a good mood.

★

Jake is meeting with his Council in Room 214. His logistics experts have an orange alert posted for Iowa. They warn Him that a pivotal vote is about to occur in the State Legislature. Jake is briefed on Republican Governor John Davis's vacillation. Jake speaks.

"We must not let Beelzie influence Governor Davis. It's that simple. We can't stop their transmissions, and they can't stop ours. Both Worlds have the same accuracy of timing, and the signals all travel at the same speed. How do we win? With copywriting!

"Holy Rollino will select the best writers in EtherWorld to pen the suggested thoughts that will be put into Governor Davis's mind. Beelzie is going to do the same. Don't forget, there are a lot of rotten dead writers. These suckers can turn a phrase, even if it is an Evil one. This is a war between copywriters. The governor has a special legislative session in six clocks. The Holy ProofReader will check all copy for typos, and the Holy CopyEditor for bad metaphors. She will give me final copy for approval. I know you will all do your best."

Unfortunately, Thomas wasn't selected to produce copy for transmission to Governor Davis. He learned of the plan from Rose, on the condition that he keep it strictly confidential. He is disappointed, not so much by the fact that he wasn't selected, but because he knows that he isn't yet a good-enough writer, let alone a great one. He will be needed for technical support, signal coordinates, intensity, and other contributions.

Rose is part of the energy group that will provide the exact wattage for maximum effect. If the beam is too strong, the governor will reject it. It would be like hearing a blaring, distorted speaker. If it's too weak, it would be like a person whispering in the back of the room, and he will pay it no attention. The wattage controls the final volume he will receive. Davis must believe they are his own thoughts.

Thomas is hoping the NetherWorld technicians lack the sophistication to be accurate. He's hoping their signal is too strong, and that the governor disregards their thought beams. Timing is also critical. A thought that is beamed too soon or too late may be totally ineffective.

★

It's eleven a.m. U.S.A. Central Time in Des Moines, Iowa. The gavel has been struck, and the special legislative session is now in order. Before the governor speaks, the president pro tem of the Iowa Senate, Psycho Fant, also a Republican, explains what's at stake and what they will be voting on.

"Today we must decide whether we will continue to let Iowa slip toward financial ruin, or will we take charge of our own future. The primary issues are labor costs and medical costs for state workers. Iowa can no longer afford the wages that teachers, police, and firefighters, to name but a few groups, are demanding. We will hear from Governor Davis. As you know, our House and Senate are roughly split evenly between Republican and Democrat. Republicans are in the slight majority. A veto by the governor will kill this program. However, his support will guarantee its passage. Your Honor, you may now have the floor."

"Thank you, Senator Psycho Fant. This isn't an easy question for us. There is much at stake, and much to be decided. I don't expect members of this august body to arrive at any snap judgments. The people of Iowa deserve our careful deliberation. I realize my vote and support is critical. I'll get right to the point and discuss the proposed cuts to police and firefighters' salaries, and the reduction of their health benefits."

Thomas and the EtherWorld team have perfect timing, and their signal is the perfect strength. The copywriters have prepared the following message, and he beams it directly into the governor's brain. Governor Davis speaks its exact words.

"To expect those among us who risk their lives every day, who prepare our children for the future, and who keep our mighty state running, to expect them to reduce the quality of their lives, and to jeopardize their health and financial well-being, is totally unacceptable. I propose instead to raise the corporate tax. There are many corporations in Iowa that don't pay one cent in taxes, due to loopholes in our tax codes. I propose tightening them up."

Governor Davis pauses for a moment. This gives Beelzie's team a chance to beam their message. Thomas's hopes are dashed. The NetherWorld transmission is perfect. It was sent a fraction of a second later than Thomas's first message and had been waiting in Davis's queue. Thomas sent his second message without knowing what Beelzie's first message was. This can be risky; without knowing the content, EtherWorld's message might be highly inappropriate. On Jake's order, Thomas sent the message anyway. Jake knew it was more important to have a positive message of any kind to counter whatever is said by the NetherWorld.

Unfortunately, Beelzie's technicians have done the same thing, and they also have messages stacked in Governor Davis's queue. He will receive and repeat them in the order they were received.

"On the other hand, my fellow Iowans, we have a golden opportunity to see our state run in the black, or in the blue if that's your color. Just think of red, white, and blue, the American flag. What's more important, the needs of the few, or the needs of the many? We can't let a small group of spoiled, overpaid civil servants dictate our financial future. They should suffer as much as the next guy. Fuck 'em!

"Iowa is at a crossroads. A wrong decision will affect our children's children. Do we want to rob them of health care, do we want their future to be one of heavy toil without rewards? We want them to walk proudly and say, 'I'm from Iowa, where what I do makes a difference. My state cares about me.'

"You know the old saying: Give a man a fish and you feed him for a day. Teach him how to fish and he will feed himself for life. That's what's happening in Iowa. All these civil servant suckers have their hands out for fucking halibut. It's time to fish or cut bait. I propose a twenty-five percent reduction in pay, and a co-pay of fifty percent on all medical and dental charges. If they don't like it, move to Kansas.

"I never fail to wonder at the golden fields of wheat and corn, and the farmers who work so hard. Iowa helps feed the world. We must make an *investment* in our citizens. Without their goodwill and their hard labor, we will have very little to show. Our society is dependent on care for everyone. Albert Schweitzer, winner of the Nobel Peace Prize, said that the quality of a culture is measured by its reverence for all life. Caring and truth are more important than manipulation for personal or corporate gain. I propose leaving all state salary and compensation packages intact. As a matter of fact, I would like to see this august body find ways to *increase* their salaries and benefits.

"Corporations are people. Iowa should be run like a corporation. Those who can produce should be allowed to produce. Those who are superfluous should be allowed to fall by the wayside. It isn't Darwinian to prop up the least among us. Let them fall through the cracks. Fuck 'em!"

There is much talking in the chamber. Senator Psycho Fant turns to speak to the senator on his left. "The poor bastard is bipolar. What do we do now?"

Both the EtherWorld and the NetherWorld realize that they have fought this battle to a draw. The governor will probably take a few days off, have a psychological evaluation, and return to work later. The vote will be postponed for several weeks, at least.

Beelzie is very happy. He informs his Generals that they went toe-to-toe with Jake and did a great job.

"Listen, youse guys, we usually get our asses kicked. Good is much stronger than Evil. Today we held our own. More like this, more like this."

Jake meets with his team in Room 214 to discuss the day's events.

"This has been a total disaster. We can't be trading thought-beams in the same person. We will drive them mad. At the same time, we must counter what Beelzie is sending. We are in a no-win situation if things continue they way they were today. If we drive a poor Human mad, Beelzie wins. If we do nothing, he will create total mayhem on Earth, and he wins. I want each of you to think about solutions to this problem."

★

Rose tells Thomas what Jake said at the briefing and passes along Jake's message that Thomas did a great job with the transmissions. It isn't his fault that the Governor appeared to be bipolar, but Thomas is downhearted.

"Rose, I feel like a failure. I very much appreciate what Jake said, but I should have figured out a way to block or jam their transmissions."

"You did your best, and........"

"No!" Thomas shouts as he interrupts Rose. "That's not good enough. I will find a way. Please excuse me."

Thomas returns to Room Total Peace, and it calms his spirit. He's acutely aware of the two sides of his nature. He can be calm, caring, and spiritual. He can also be a New York punk. A New York punk......hmmmmm.

Thomas leaves Room TP and glides to see Rose.

"I have an idea. Can Jake contact Beelzie directly?"

"Yes, he can, by missal."

"What! You mean a guided missile?"

"No, it's like one of those canisters in bank tubes at the drive-up windows. The missals land outside Rooms 214 and 213. They are rarely sent, only a few per Earth decade. What's your idea?"

"Good is stronger than Evil, correct? Beelzie and his Generals are strong in the NetherWorld. The Composites are fierce in the NetherWorld, but get them outside in Free Space and they ain't so tough. Here's what we do. I suggest Jake and Holy Rollino propose a peace conference in the Neutral Territory. An equal number of participants from each side will attend. We capture all of his delegation and put them in a Containment Room. End of problem."

"Oh Thomas, Jake will never agree to that. Everyone knows you can't hold the Devil. I'll mention your suggestion, just the same."

Rose introduces Thomas's idea at the next Room 214 briefing. Jake and Holy Rollino confer in private for a few micro clocks, then Jake speaks with Rose.

"Please go get Thomas and tell him to bring his polarized sunglasses. He may be onto something."

Rose is extremely excited and tells Thomas that he is summoned to Room 214. She's proud of him and holds his arm as they walk into the room. Jake speaks.

"Thomas, tell me more about your idea for a peace conference. You suggest kidnapping them and putting them in a Containment Room?"

"Yes Sir, much as you did with the Evil Beings in Room S. You put a huge steel ball around them so they can't escape."

"That's a good plan, but Beelzie cannot be contained in *any* area. He has the power to escape at will. There is something else we can do, though. I'm going to propose a peace conference in neutral territory, at Ray's Pizzeria in Andromeda. We will threaten Beelzie with force, and an Intergalactic War he cannot win, if he continues his behavior. He would lose all of Sector F, and possibly part of Sector G.

"We are gentle Beings, but highly fierce when fighting for the Good. His Generals are basically mush. If we can put the fear of Jake in them, we will really cramp their style. Very well done, Thomas. I want you and Rose to be part of our delegation. I'll prepare a missal for Beelzie."

17

Jake personally composes the message that he will send to Beelzie. He reads it aloud to his staff.

"Beelzie, the time has come when you must fight for your survival. If you continue to destroy Human life, in direct violation of the Prime Directive, we will have no choice but to destroy NetherWorld. A protracted war will do neither of us any good. I urge you to remember the last war. The Archangel Gabriel kicked your asses. I promise you it *will* happen again. I propose a peace conference. We will each bring one other Supreme Being and twelve additional Beings. You have two choices: either we have this conference, or you will be attacked. It's that simple. I propose that we hold it in Neutral Territory, at Ray's Pizzeria in Andromeda. For your own safety, I strongly suggest that you do not come heavy."

The missal is sent to the basket outside Room 213 and is immediately brought to Beelzie. He calls the Generals to order in the banquet room.

"Listen, youse guys. We may have gone too far with the poor dear governor of Iowa. I told you we done good, but maybe too good. We don't want to risk direct confrontation with Jake and the EtherWorld. We can have much more fun if we don't have to watch our backs all the time. I'm going to

234

accept his offer. Hun and Chopper, you will be my numbers two and three. I want Diphtheria sitting next to me. She's a great distraction. I can't wait to see those Holy eyes sneaking peeks down her tunic, instead of paying attention to the conference. Hun, select the other Generals. Make sure your uniforms are pressed and your medals polished."

Beelzie writes his return message to Jake and puts it in the missal.

"Dearest Jake and the mild-mannered EtherWorld wimps: We are not afraid of you. Not one tiny little bit. You vastly overestimate your strength. However, a protracted war, as you put it, would be somewhat boring and not fit in with our entertainment plans. I will bring my numbers two and three, plus twelve others who will be happy to show you their hospitality. Don't you come heavy, either, or some of your hand-picked cuties will be carried home in pine boxes. I propose eleven clocks from now. Ray's Pizzeria is acceptable, especially since Al and Lucky will be with our team. It's not a good idea to get them angry. I can't wait to see you crawl in public."

Jake reads between the lines and knows that Beelzie is scared. He reads the message to his Staff.

"Sounds like a battleship mouth and a rowboat ass to me," Thomas says, *slightly* improving his ability to make a metaphor.

235

In his message, Beelzie stated that he is bringing *two* of his top Bubs. Jake will do the same. In addition to his number three, Holy Rollino, he chooses his number two, Sonny. It will be Jake, Sonny, and Holy Rollino, the Holy Ghostwriter. Sonny is especially tough. He casts thieves out of temples and is the most feared Being in the NetherWorld. They will cower at the mere sight of him. Holy Rollino thinks it's a great idea.

Sonny and Holy Rollino select the team of twelve for the Peace Conference:

Rose von Kolisch
Thomas Buchetta
Fiorello LaGuardia
Frank Sinatra
Joe DiMaggio
Michelangelo Buonarroti
Bobby Darin Cassoto
Arturo Toscanini
Lorenzo de Medici
Vince Lombardi
Giuseppe Garibaldi
Dean Martin

Jake is impressed that Rose is the only non-Italian chosen by Sonny and Holy Rollino.

There is a strategy meeting called by Room 214 in the next clock. Thomas is the only one in the Room wearing polarized sunglasses. Rose sits next to him. Thomas is very nervous and makes small-talk.

"I didn't know there was a Ray's Pizzeria in Andromeda."

Holy Rollino says, "There are Ray's Pizzerias everywhere in the Universe. There's one in the Cartwheel Galaxy, the Cigar Galaxy, the Comet Galaxy, the Sombrero Galaxy, the Pinwheel Galaxy, the Sunflower Galaxy, not to mention M82 and M87. That's one Hell of a franchise."

"How come they never opened one in our Milky Way?"

"They refused to pay the protection money Room 214 demanded."

★

The Holy Trio fine-tunes their EtherWorld strategy. It's pretty straightforward, with no surprises. They are going to play hardball. Thomas suggests a backup plan. Jake asks him what he has in mind.

"Yes Sir, thank you for asking, Sir. I know that we agreed to have only twelve of us plus Your Holy Selves at the actual peace conference, but we didn't say that some of our best people would not also be in the general area. I suggest a squadron of Top Gun ArchAngels be hidden inside the Food 'n' Sex Restaurant. That's the last place Beelzie will look. He won't connect us with that kind of establishment. They can move out quickly on your signal in case Beelzie comes heavy."

"Thomas, that would be a deception. Although we didn't specifically say we *weren't* going to bring additional ArchAngel power, that still violates the spirit of the peace conference. Let's do it anyway, good idea. Sonny, you take care of that; you've trained the best fighters."

While the EtherWorld is finalizing its plans, Beelzie and his Bubs are combing over last-minute details.

"Okay, listen up. Here's what we're gonna do. If those wimps think we are not going to come heavy, they don't know anything about the Devil. We *never* do what we say we're gonna do. They are so trusting. It's so disgusting. Hey, that rhymes. Their trust is so very convenient. Chopper, you will pay an early visit to Ray's Pizzeria. Bring one dozen of your finest Damascus steel, double-edged swords. Take three sacks of Roman gold and give them to Ray's manager. Make him an offer he can't refuse. Pay him off, then take the swords and hide them in the men's room, above the toilets. Tell the manager if he says anything to the wimps, you will personally see that he is ground up and served on one of his pizzas.

"If the conference doesn't go exactly the way we want it to, we are all going to have to pee at the same time. When we come out of the men's room swinging and slashing with those swords, Jake will have to agree to our demands, or his precious wimps will be diced like celery stalks, metaphorically speaking, of course."

Hun suggests they hide Composites in the Andromeda Galaxy, and jump the wimps after they leave.

"Not a good idea, Hun. Composites are slower than Orcs in Open Space. We would need thousands of them to do the job, and that many would be seen by the wimps. What we *could* do is assign a few hundred EUS Extreme Ultimate Slime Beings. They are masters of disguise and are very fast. We can plant them in areas all around Ray's. They can morph into waiters, delivery men, traffic cops, and toll-booth Beings. We can arm them with powerful .45 caliber Atomizer-Dissolver-Vaporizers. They can carry these hidden in violin cases. The EtherWorld wimps will think they are a Holy orchestra. Hun, you make that happen."

★

Beelzie and the Bubs march into the conference room in perfect lockstep, with high leg-kicks. Beelzie barks the commands. "Right face! Sit down!" All the chairs are pulled out at the exact same split second. Jake's team counters with another unique entrance that is designed to rattle Beelzie. They all have their hands in their pockets and walk very slowly around the entire restaurant before sitting down.

There is some confusion over who will sit where. Finally, Beelzie admits that where they sit has already been decided by historical precedent. Obviously, he is to sit at the left end of the table and his Bubs on the left side. And Jake is to sit at the right end with his staff on the right side. The table is only four feet wide, so the two teams glare at each other like territory-guarding tomcats, each waiting for the other to flinch. (The omniscient narrator also has trouble with metaphors.)

"If I may, I would like to begin our discussions by making a very simple statement," Beelzie says. "All negotiations involve give and take. You are willing to give up something, and you want something in return. I might ask the EtherWorld, since youse called this peace conference, what it is you wish to give up, and what it is you want in return."

Jake doesn't intend to speak first; he wants Beelzie to commit himself. He dodges the question.

"That's a good point we will have to discuss. However, we have not had our pizza. No negotiations can begin while the table is bare."

The EtherWorld team orders Chianti Ruffino and the NetherWorld team red bourbon. They do not share food or drink. The EtherWorld orders pizzas with sausage, mushrooms, peppers, garlic, ground beef, anchovies, and other delights. You don't want to know the toppings on the NetherWorld pizzas.

Diphtheria says hello to Thomas and tells him she really enjoyed visiting his Room. She thanks him for all those great new sex positions. "Why don't you glide up and see me sometime? We can try a few of them out before I put them in my book." Rose glares at Thomas, who wishes he could crawl under the table.

He whispers to Rose, "Nothing happened, I swear."

Rose continues to glare at him.

Jake begins the discussion. "It's really very simple, Beelzie. If you send any more continuous transmissions into the same Human, I'm going to squash you like a cockroach. Your Generals will be your pallbearers."

"You can't do that, Jake, I'm already dead."

"I will make you more dead, even deader than dead. If you think EtherWorld lacks guts, wait until you see what we have in mind for you when you lose this war. Beelzie, you have no class."

"Jake, Jake, you talk about class. How is it showing class when you make threats before the specifics of our peace conference are even discussed? Don't you see how your eager aggression masks an unsure position? Sonny is supposed to be the Prince of Peace, yet he stares at me like he wants to cut my head off."

"Yes, he's the Prince of Peace, and I'm also a peaceful Supreme Being, but woe to goblins and ghouls who disturb my favorite TV shows."

"TV shows?"

"Yes, TV shows. You've done it many times."

"Aha, now we're getting somewhere. So, Jake, it is proposed by you that all activity, transmissions, wars and the like, do not occur during your favorite TV shows. I have no trouble with that. See, we have already agreed on something."

"Smoke and mirrors, smoke and mirrors, Beelzie. You're good at it. I have a simple and direct question. There can be no multiple choice, snow jobs, social studies essays, long-winded claptrap of any kind here. Do you, yes or no, intend to stop multiple transmissions into Humans?"

"Thank you for your question, Jake. If I say yes, what will you offer in return?"

"We will let you go back to your shit-hole with your private parts intact."

"I must question the good faith of your intentions. Throughout this conference you have been discourteous, rude, and quite dismissive of us and our position."

Vince Lombardi turns to Chopper and tells him he's very ugly. "Let me tell you something, Saber Tooth. Since I've been in the EtherWorld, I've never lost a football game. You think you're tough. Compared to a Green Bay Packers lineman, you are a pussy-whipped dildo. I refuse to lose, you got that?"

Al Capone answers Vince. "There are some of us who don't need to go face to face and butt helmets like billy goats. We have a different method. Nothing beats a Tommy gun fired from a moving car. We'll see how many touchdowns you can score with holes in your ass."

Frank Sinatra shakes his head in disappointment. "You know, Al, it's guys like you and Lucky who have given Italians a bad name. It would have been much better if the two of you had never lived. There is a distinct possibility that an alteration to your virtual selves can be arranged for both of you in the AfterWorld. My advice to the both of you is to hide. Sheesh, what Neanderthals."

Sonny stands up and moves toward Beelzie. All the Generals get up from the table and run to the corner of the restaurant in fear.

Beelzie excuses himself, runs from the table, and claims that he has to take a piss. The rest of the Bubs follow him. Thomas suggests that Jake activate the Top Gun ArchAngels, and Jake does so.

Beezlie and the Bubs come roaring out of the men's room with Damascus steel swords swinging violently above their heads. Jake and his team calmly draw Smith & Wesson Model 60 .375 magnum revolvers, loaded with Buffalo bore 125 grain hollow-point bullets, that were hidden in their tunics. Beelzie and the Bubs stop their advance cold and stand motionless.

"Sorry, Beelzie, looks like you brought swords to a gunfight."

"No fair! No fair!" Beelzie whines. "You came heavy!"

At that moment the EUS, Extreme Ultimate Slime Beings, crash through the door and surround Jake and his team. The Top Gun ArchAngels arrive a micro-clock later and surround the Slime Beings.

Thomas has an idea. From out of nowhere he says, "This is a Mexican standoff."

"What's that?" Beelzie asks.

"That's when each side is so strong that no one dares to initiate violence. It's sort of like the Cold War between the Soviet Union and the United States. All that nuclear might pointed at each other guaranteed peace."

This idea of war bringing peace appeals to Beelzie, and Jake sees a way to turn Thomas's idea to his advantage.

"Beelzie, here's what I propose. Since mutual destruction is very bad for the complexion, we each limit our thought beams into Humans to one per day per Human. You can send anything you want, without letting us know what it is.

In other words, we won't monitor you. We will also send one thought beam per day per Human. You don't monitor us."

"Why should we agree to that?"

"Think of the consequences if you don't. Sonny is riled. In a few minutes he will cast you all out into an unimaginable horror, deep into the dark recesses of an ugly wormhole. You will be thrown so far away, you will have to turn south to go north."

"Let's try it for a while." Beelzie swallows hard and is the first to flinch. "But how do we know Thomas won't try to monitor or intercept our transmissions?"

"You have my word on it."

"For Christ's sake, Jake. I'm the Devil. I take nobody at their word. I need real, concrete, tangible guarantees."

"That's easy. You can tell if we are monitoring you if we counter your transmissions with an antidote. We are both going to let the Human Beings decide for themselves. Neither of us will be allowed to force their behavior. They must exercise their own free will." They formally end the conference on that agreement.

★

"*Why don't you glide up and see me sometime? We can try a few of them out before I put them in my book.*" Rose mimics Diphtheria. "You are full of surprises. How could you? She smells like rotting cabbage."

"Oh, I don't know. I kind of like it. It's an earthy odor. Reminds me of those times I really wanted to get down and dirty."

"You're not going to shock me, Thomas. I know you're full of....."

"Just one moment here, Dr. von Kolisch! Do you remember, way back when I was an Initiate, I asked you about the Swirl you attended. You told me that in the EtherWorld, everyone loves everyone, but the details are private. You said we don't kiss and tell. Is there a slight contradiction here? What's good for the goose is good for the....."

"Jerk Being!"

"I already told you that nothing happened. Why don't you believe me? I do not lie. I was trapped in Room CS in the NetherWorld and Hon brought her in. She's an EUS Being, and I didn't want to end up in tiny pieces. So I diverted her from ugly, kinky sex to watching an American porn station from Earth. She photographed the sex positions for inclusion in her book. I wonder if she's going to publish it and where it will be available. I can get you a copy if you'd like."

"Jerk Being!"

246

"A truly Enlightened Soul will admit it when she's wrong."

"Modified Jerk Being. Thomas, as soon as we get back home from Andromeda, Jake wants all of us in Room 214 for a debriefing."

"Wow, did you ever change the subject as fast as you could."

Rose gives Thomas a toothy grin.

A few clocks later, Room 214 fills up for Jake's debriefing.

Saint Peter has been summoned as a trusted advisor. "Come va, Gregorio?" he says to Jake.

"Cosi, cosi, Pietro," Jake responds. "E si?"

"Bene," Saint Peter replies.

Thomas whispers to Rose. "Why did Saint Peter call Jake *Gregorio*?"

"I don't know."

The debriefing lasts for only a short while, because everyone is tired. They decide to place every available monitor facing the NetherWorld. If a violation is detected, they are readying plans for punitive action. As the meeting breaks up, Thomas approaches Saint Peter.

"Saint Peter, Sir, I have a question for you. Why did you call Jake *Gregorio*?"

"You don't know why? I'll tell you. His full name is Gregorio DiGiacomo. You just call him Jake for short."

"You mean He's Italian?"

"Yes."

"Holy Spumoni!" Thomas is all excited. "You mean the Holy Trio is composed of three Italians?"

"Si, that is correct. There's Gregorio DiGiacomo, Sonny, and Holy Rollino. I hope that isn't a problem for you."

"No wonder the basilica of Saint Peter's is so big. You have a direct connection. I was curious why there are so many large churches in Italy, and why Vatican City is located there. Now I know."

"Rose, you are not going to believe this, but the Holy Trio is all Italian."

"Oh!" Rose is mildly surprised. "No wonder we always have cannoli at our meetings."

"That's Holy Cannoli to you, Dr. Rose von Kolisch."

18

Beelzie is emboldened by NetherWorld's performance at the peace conference. He addresses the Bubs in the banquet hall.

"Listen up, youse guys. Now is not the time to relax. Yes, we did real good in Andromeda. Ray's Pizzeria will never be the same. We fought them to a draw, and they can't stop us from transmitting. Now is the time to strike again, while they are analyzing and quantifying, like all hesitant incompetents will do.

"Here's what's going down. Chopper, I want you to select the one hundred nastiest Beings in the NetherWorld. They need to have a rank of EUS or higher. Select morphers, drillers, killers, and logistical computer support.

"Your goal is Room S. That's where all the Evil Beings are kept. No one knows anything about them except Jake. He hasn't even informed the Enlightened Beings on Room 214 staff what's inside. Room S should be in the NetherWorld, not the EtherWorld. It's like having Guantanamo Naval Base in Cuba. Those Beings need to be liberated.

"Chopper, you take your team and drill a hole right into the heart of the huge steel ball. You are to liberate those majestic creatures. Can you imagine the mayhem this will cause as they slither around the EtherWorld? Right after you free the beasts, you hotfoot it back here. You have my permission, indeed you have my blessing, to destroy anyone who gets in your way. Jake threatened us with war, and he just might get his wish."

Chopper is so happy, he is in tears.

The raiding party glides slowly across the border from Sector F. Although they are all cloaked, Thomas reads an energy spike from Sector E. He's not yet sure what's going on, so he doesn't sound the Y·O·J alarm. He does call Room 214, and speaks directly to Jake.

"Thomas, I know Beelzie. I fully expected him to launch more dirty work soon after the conference ended. He thinks we will be complacent. Let me know where you read the energy burst, and the exact clock it passes each location."

"Yes, Sir," Thomas says. He tracks the energy field and plots the coordinates from where they originated, and their last two known locations. He then knows their heading. He extends the line from those known points outward, and plots their destination.

"Sir, they're headed right for Room S. Should I sound the alarm?"

"Not yet. Let them proceed for now. Stay alert to sound the alarm in a short while. Tell every Being to find pink paint."

Chopper and the Bubs arrive at Room S. The drillers use NetherWorld carbide-tip technology to bore into the steel sphere. It's taking many clocks, because the metal is so hard. Chopper is concerned that their cloaking devices will wear off soon. Finally, he hears a loud hissing sound.

One hundred snakes pour from the drilled hole in a slithery wave. It's common knowledge among wildlife biologists that a baby duck will imprint on the first thing it sees. The duckling thinks it's his mama. These snakes do the same thing, but not because they think they recognize their mama. It is because they have found lunch. They follow the first Being they see until they catch it and swallow it whole. The snake gets bigger and bigger with each Being it devours. Not too far from the Sombrero Galaxy, there was a snake slightly over one light-year long. Sonny finally chopped its head off. He hates snakes.

They are very fast and can grab their tails with their mouths and roll at warp speed. Chopper was the very first to be swallowed whole. The rest of the raiding party, now uncloaked, is also devoured.

Jake sends out the alarm, JOY! JOY! JOY! He gives instructions to all Sectors and all Beings to round up the snakes. They will not swallow anyone who is a Republican, so Jake instructs all the pursuers to paint pink elephants on their clothes. There were one hundred snakes in Room S, and ninety-nine have been captured. Throughout the EtherWorld, they search and search for number one hundred, but to no avail. Finally, Thomas picks up a snake trail.

"It's headed to Earth, Sir, to Texas, in the U.S.A. Should we follow it, Sir?"

"No, Thomas, let it go. Once they are on Earth, they lose all their power and are no different from any other boa constrictor. He's trying to find a home. He's trying to find a kindred spirit."

The snake is finally at peace. It wound up being the personal pet of George W. Bush. Now it sleeps every night happily curled up at the foot of his bed.

★

Jake informs Beelzie, via missal, that his raiding team has been swallowed by the snake creatures they liberated. The snakes have been recaptured and placed in a much larger and stronger containment ball. No known drill or cutting torch can penetrate it. Chopper and his Bubs are in the bellies of the snakes and will be allowed to dissolve. They will not be returned.

Beelzie is told that no further action will be forthcoming against the NetherWorld, since many of his high-ranking Beings no longer exist. Jake ends his message with a very important philosophical warning: "When you use your own hand to destroy, you will bring about your own destruction."

Another meeting is called by Beelzie in the banquet hall. This time the Generals are absent, except for Hun. The other chairs are filled with Politicians, Liars, Frauds, and all manner of Cheats and Swindlers. Beelzie makes one of his best speeches.

"Okay, youse guys. First of all, I would like to apologize to all of you for a policy that is completely wrong and corrupt. I've been giving it serious thought, and Jake is entirely correct. He told me, and I quote, 'When you use your own hand to destroy, you will bring about your own destruction.' Every time we mix it up with EtherWorld, we lose. The reason I asked all of you here is that the NetherWorld will embark on a total paradigm shift, and I want you all to be part of it. We will no longer try to get the Humans to kill each other, or unleash natural disasters like tsunamis, volcanoes, and tornadoes upon them. We are working against ourselves."

There is much murmuring among those present, and Beelzie sees that they are very uncomfortable. However, they are smart enough not to speak out loud, because the chef is standing by the door. He has a grin on his face, and he holds one twelve-inch-long Sabatier deboning knife in each hand.

"We want Humans to be happy, for now. We are going to beam thoughts into them that they should live long and prosper. We want them to go forth and multiply.

"Oh yes, muthafucka!" Beelzie shouts. "We want them to multiply. That is the solution to our problems. If we can't win the war for control of Human minds, we will simply let them do what they please. They will bring about their own destruction for sure. Listen, youse guys, I've done a lot of research here. We have some friends on Earth. Former President George W. Bush said the science of global warming was junk science. Listen to his remark at the G-8 Summit in Japan in 2008. I quote, 'Goodbye from the world's biggest polluter.' He punched the air and grinned widely, as British Minister Gordon Brown and French President Nicolas Sarkozy looked on in disbelief. He also said on May 12, 2008, 'I'll be long gone before some smart person ever figures out what happened inside this Oval Office.'

"I have great news for you, President Bush: Your dream has come true. I know you were talking to me. I know what went on inside your oval office. Bush is a good man, a very good man.

"Former Vice President Dan Quayle once said, 'It isn't pollution that's harming the environment. It's the impurities in our air and water that are doing it.' With men like these in high places, how can we lose? They are both Republicans, by the way.

"We all leave a legacy behind. George Bush has instructed many people in the NetherWorld Way. President Obama, a so-called Democrat, in September, 2011 blocked the Environmental Protection Agency from implementing an enforceable smog standard. He bypassed the head of his own EPA, who warned him that his stance was scientifically and legally indefensible. Obama defied the Clean Air Act and a Supreme Court decision. He said jobs are more important than Human health or survival of the Earth. But, most of all, he wants to be reelected, because his approval rating is in the toilet. I'm proud of his decision.

"An important milestone was reached in October, 2011. Human population reached seven billion. This is wonderful. We will send positive thoughts to all those striving people in developing counties. We will beam messages to Humans in India, China, Brazil, Mexico, all of Africa and Asia. One Human at a time, we will teach them how great it is to have many lovely children crawling around on the rugs. Big families are necessary for communal security. We will make them lust to own a Lincoln Navigator and a five-foot-wide flat-screen TV. We will tell them they have as much right to use oil and electricity as the Americans do. Overpopulation is the root of all pollution and environmental degradation, and the root of all Evil.

"There are two things working for us. One, Humans are breeding like rabbits. Planned Parenthood doesn't stand a chance. Two, all this pollution and energy use from transportation and the production of material goods will ultimately doom the planet. If we can't win the battle against the EtherWorld directly, we will win it by default."

The Politicians, Liars, Frauds, and all manner of Cheats and Swindlers give Beelzie a standing ovation. When they slam their tankards down on the table, not one is in perfect time. The chef jumps up and down with delight, thinking he has so many people to prepare. Beelzie shakes his head no, and instead orders the sous chef to prepare the chef for dessert.

Beelzie continues, "Thank you, thank you very much. It's important that we don't make this transition too abruptly. We will launch a few raids by Sacrificial Composites, and beam hateful messages to key Humans. We will gradually phase this activity out, over a period of one Earth year. The change will be so subtle, I doubt even the geniuses in EtherWorld will catch on before it's too late.

"Hun, it's time for you to put away your sword. You don't want to end up like Chopper, in the belly of a snake. Grab a suit and tie and join the U.S. Chamber of Commerce. You will do far greater damage if you support their policies than you ever could with an entire army. Our methods have been too primitive. It's time we modernize."

★

Thomas has gotten another citation from EtherWay Transit Security for a too-loud muffler. He is forced to plug in the baffles to quiet down his Mustang SlingShot. He wonders how Janis is able to get so much speed from her Mercedes without making a racket. *Must be German engineering.* He drives to Gabriel's Hideaway for a wee nip. He doesn't see any of the regulars this evening but does spy a familiar figure sitting at the South bar. He introduces himself.

"Hello, President Reagan. My name is Thomas Buchetta. Sir, I thought you lived across the border in Sector R."

"I'm one of the very few who is called a Swing Being. I can freely travel across the border from Sector R to Gabriel's Hideaway. This was Jake's idea. He said it was important for others to interact with me to learn what not to do to the average working Human."

"That's right, Mr. President. You did break the Air Traffic Controllers Union. American labor never really recovered, and collective bargaining is almost dead. Many people are suffering as a result. Don't you feel bad about that decision?"

"No, Thomas, I don't. No one appreciates that fact that I smited the Evil Empire and won the Cold War."

"History books tell us, Mr. President, that it was Russian Premier Gorbachev who dissolved the former Soviet Union, rather than bankrupt his people with outrageous defense spending. The books tell us that American money won the Cold War. You had nothing to do with it, sir."

"The books lie. My contribution was immense. I promise you that nobody will ever forget *Bedtime for Bonzo*. I will forever be 'Old Boraxo.' That is something you can never be. To this day, whenever my name is mentioned at Conservative conventions, the faithful get misty-eyed. I'm a hero to them. What do you have to show for your life?"

"I joined the Script Writers Union, and paid my dues regularly, even though I was poor. Weren't you a member of the Actors Guild?"

"I'm going to end this discussion now, Buchetta. I have more important things to do across the border."

Thomas did not enjoy his conversation with Former President Reagan. He spots two more historical figures sitting at the bar.

"Excuse me, ma'am. Aren't you Amelia Earhart? And you, sir, must be Captain Fred Noonan. I'm Thomas Buchetta. There is so much mystery surrounding your disappearance over the South Pacific."

"We don't usually talk about it. It's great to be here. The flying machines are much safer. We have a Ford Tri-motor SlingShot. It has great range and never runs out of fuel."

"I hope I'm not being a pain asking you questions. It's such a treat to meet Humans I've read about. How did you crash? Did you run out of fuel? Was it a mechanical breakdown? I always wondered if the two of you were lovers, if I may be so bold as to inquire. You are together here."

"What do you think we were doing in the Enola Gay before it crashed? So, now you know. There was no room in that old Lockheed Model 10 Electra. Move in the wrong direction, and pow, you hit the aileron control. It was worth it, though." Noonan winks at Earhart.

Thomas is enjoying his living history lesson. He notices an underage young woman sitting at a table near the center fountain. She's very pretty and immediately catches his eye. Although she seems no more than sixteen years old, she has a small glass of vodka, and she's eating a piece of Uzbekistan sweet walnut brittle.

"Hello, I'm Thomas Buchetta. What is your name?"

"I am Anastasia Nikolaevna. So pleased to meet you. Do sit down."

"Are you the Anastasia of legend? Are you the long-lost Princess of the Romanov family? Wow, there have been dozens of movies and countless books written about you."

"Don't forget, there was also a song about me sung by Pat Boone. It was so horrible I almost came back from the dead to smash all the records. Then there was that imposter, Anna Anderson. She wasn't even Russian! How gullible you Americans are. There were dozens of people who claimed to be me. All of them were mentally ill. Your country is full of nut cases who want five minutes of media fame. They will do anything to get it."

"Anastasia, did you survive the massacre and die of natural causes?"

"Oh, such a pleasant subject. Thomas, you are not subtle. No, I was killed by the Bolshevik Secret Police on July 17, 1918 in Tsarskoye Selo. My body is buried 200 feet away from the rest of my family. If you don't mind, I would like to talk about something else. Have you no consideration?"

"I'm very sorry. It's just that I always wanted to know. Would you like to go for a ride in my Mustang SlingShot?"

"No. You have no tact. You are not romantic, just curious. Please excuse me, I must go."

Thomas knows he didn't handle that well. He may be curious, but there are limits to how much he can invade a Being's privacy. He can't resist unlocking the secrets of the past. He's thinking about writing a book on the subject. Is the past the key to the future? How much of the Enlightened Being we become in the EtherWorld owes its roots to the Earth Being. Is it nature or nurture? It seems to him that people remain themselves at their core, but can change many aspects of their personalities by embracing new thoughts. He realizes he still has free will. He can make decisions for Good or Evil. As he progresses toward Enlightenment, he finds it easier to make the Good decisions.

★

Thomas glides to the Stratosphere above Ormond Beach, Florida. He learned from monitoring one of Cindy's cell conversations with Piranha that his parents have retired and moved from Vermont to Florida. They are both sad to have lost their sons. He knows he can send one message to each of them, but doesn't know what to say or how to say it. They seem happy enough, although his father is restless without work to do.

He picks up another Being on the EtherReceiver scan of his parent's house. It's Cindy. All of a sudden his virtual blood pressure climbs sky high. He pinpoints her coordinates in his crosshairs like a fighter pilot who has spotted an enemy plane. (His metaphors are improving.) He uses the fine-tuner to separate out the thought patterns and listens to all three. Cindy must have been there for quite a while, and is now leaving. Thomas has missed most of her conversation.

"Bye Cindy, thanks for stopping by and thanks for the gift. This means a lot to us. We will never have to worry about money ever again. Wow! She gave us one million dollars," he hears his mother say.

What is that, guilt money? He thinks out loud. *Why the hell would she want to do that? It's completely out of character. I'll bet it was an EtherWorld message from Rose.*

He convinces himself he has the answer. *I've got it. I could never give my parents that kind of money. Now Cindy's making them rich to rub their faces in the fact that she's the success and I was a failure.*

Rose would tell me that I'm just jealous. Perhaps she's right. I'm getting out of here.

Thomas returns to Room Renaissance and says hello to Boots and Tabitha. Tabitha is pregnant, and Thomas is once again jealous. He opens two cans of gourmet kitty tuna. The cats humor him by saying meow, instead of their normal abstract, deep metaphysical conversation. Both cats have Thomas well trained.

He leaves them alone and checks a computer printout. It's a linear graph of a week's worth of scans on his EtherReceiver. He notices a slight reduction in negative energy emanating from across the border. There is something about the graph that disturbs him.

A week later, he prints another scan. Again, there is a reduction in negative energy. He links the two scans and notices that there is the same daily reduction of energy. There is one-tenth of one percent per day decrease, without deviation. He doesn't know what this means, or if it's significant. Thomas supposes he should be thankful that the negative energy isn't increasing. He will continue to monitor it.

19

*T*here is a welcome calm in the AfterWorld. Outright hostilities from Beelzie have diminished. It's time for the weekly status meeting in Room 214. Once again, Thomas is asked to participate and to present a report on NetherWorld energy fields and thought transmissions.

Rose has had a promotion and moved up one chair, and she no longer has to do purchasing, inventory, and auditing. The Room slowly fills up, and everyone is in a jovial mood. Rose tells Thomas about the promotion.

"That's great, Rose! Congratulations. Who will be doing your job?"

"Hiya, hon!" Janis says, peeking over her tiny gold-rimmed glasses. "I guess that would be me. Hope I can learn the job. I have no trouble being the Music Director, but auditing and accounting are not my bag."

"Bernie Madoff didn't know much about them either, and he got quite rich. But of course, he was thrown in jail."

Thomas's sense of humor is appreciated by the staff. Food is brought in for the group. Instead of cannoli and spumoni, the trays are full of rugelach, braided challah, cinnamon babkas, and bagels with smoked salmon, tomatoes, onion, and cream cheese.

"Where's the cannoli?" Thomas asks. "This is rugelach."

"That's Holy Rugelach to you, Mr. Buchetta. This is Kosher food!" Rose is all excited. "Wow! Very neat!"

A large bearded man enters the room.

"All right already. Let's come to order. Jake will be on vacation for a few months for a much-deserved rest. I will be taking over as number one. My name is Jehovah. Let's not talk business until we eat. Rose, please pass the rugelach. Come on, eat, eat, eat!"

Thomas whispers to Rose. "Looks like we have a Holy Quartet." Rose gives him a wide grin.

"I would like to welcome Janis to our staff. Hello, Thomas Buchetta, I haven't met you yet. I've heard good things about your electronics work. If you were still on Earth, I'd loan you some money to start your own company. So, Thomas, since you are the center of attention at this moment, why don't you give us an update on old Lucifer Pants."

"Thank you, Holy Jehovah, Sir. I really don't have much to report, except a slight reduction in negative energy from 'Lucifer Pants,' as you call him." Thomas laughs out loud when he says the name. "There is one minor thing I probably should mention, and..."

"And and and, yes yes yes. It's the minor things that can foretell major events. What do you see, Thomas?"

"In the past few weeks, there has been a systematic reduction in NetherWorld energy. The same one-tenth of one percent drop per day. That doesn't sound like a random loss. It has to be planned. I have no idea what it means."

"Neither do I, but I promise you that Lucy Pants is up to something. We know he's a no-goodnik. What proof do we need further? I'll tell you. None! We have to take it as a given that it does mean something rotten, and we have to find out what."

Saint Peter walks into the room.

"Come va, Jovanni?" he asks Jehovah.

"Cosi, cosi, Pietro," Jehovah responds. "E si?"

"Bene. Sorry I'm late. The Red Sox were playing the Yankees in the playoffs, and I wanted to see the end of the game."

"What was the final score?" Jehovah asks.

"Yankees seven and Red Sox three."

"Excellent!" says Jehovah, who is an ardent Yankees fan.

Half the Room cheers, while the other half boos. Thomas boos the loudest. Unlike Beelzie's banquet hall get-togethers, Beings can disagree in Room 214 without being handed to the chef.

"Pietro, that gives me an idea." Jehovah suggests another Game Week since there are no pressing events that require constant attention. The meeting breaks up, and Janis invites Rose, Thomas, and some of her new friends to Gabriel's Hideaway.

Rose stops Saint Peter as he is leaving. "Saint Peter, Sir."

"Yes, Rose?"

"Why did you call Jehovah *Jovanni*?"

"You don't know? I thought everyone knew. His full name is Jovanni Benedetto. He's from Bologna."

"But I thought he was Jewish, the Hebrew God of Israel."

"Of course he's Jewish. He *is* the Hebrew God of Israel. He's an Italian Jew. He and Sonny are best friends. They played bocce together when they were kids."

★

Holy Rollino and his staff are busy in Room FT, Football Tickets, printing this week's lottery. Now that the baseball season is drawing to a close, most of the games are college

266

and professional football. Fifty teams who play each other are listed, and there is a blank space before each pairing. You are supposed to write in the final score in that space. For example, if you think the Giants are going to beat the Redskins by a score of 21 to 7, you circle the Giants and write 21 to 7 in the blank space. Since there are so many people playing, it isn't unusual for some Beings to successfully pick all fifty winners. The winning tickets are scanned, and the Being who comes closest to the actual total point spread is the overall winner. The tickets are free, so everyone plays. The expenses are part of Room 214's operating budget.

Each player has a chance to win something. If you pick more than seventy-five percent of the winners, you get a box of one dozen fresh-baked rugelach. If you predict them all correctly, your prize is a custom-made silk embroidered yarmulke. If you're the grand-prize winner, you are Jehovah's special guest at Gabriel's Hideaway, usually to watch a baseball game. Let me tell you, you have never seen food like what they serve when Jehovah throws a party.

The contest is open to all Beings, whether or not they are Enlightened. Many Sector E Beings have gotten transferred to a higher Sector once they have won the grand prize. No one has more influence in the EtherWorld than Jehovah. He expanded the lottery ticket program that Saint Peter started in 1955. It is administered in Room 214 by the Director of Gambling. To keep the game clean, the tickets are printed and distributed by Beings in Sector A.

Tabitha is a mitten-toed cat, so she can easily grasp a pencil. When Thomas isn't looking, she and Boots fill out the lottery ticket. Boots is excellent at choosing winners, especially the Vermont Catamounts, Arizona Wildcats, Carolina Panthers, Detroit Lions, and Detroit Tigers. After they complete their selections, they both put paw prints at the bottom to identify themselves. Boots carries the ticket in his mouth to Thomas and asks him to turn it in when he passes by Room 214.

"Sure, Boots, you've won more prizes than I have."

★

There is a special meeting of the Holy Women's Auxiliary in Room 214. As he was leaving, Thomas noticed the posting. It listed those who would be in attendance, including The Virgin Mary. No time was given for the meeting.

"Rose, do you know what day and time the Holy Women's Auxiliary is meeting in Room 214?"

"Why do you want to know?"

"I'm just curious if they will meet at the same clock we do."

"They meet in sixteen micro-clocks. That's three micro-clocks earlier than we do."

"Thanks, Rose."

Thomas has an idea. Since the Virgin Mary will be occupied for quite a while at her meeting, he is going to sneak back into Room W and try to make it with Marilyn Monroe and/or Jayne Mansfield. He anxiously watches the micro-clock and moves out from his place at the scheduled time.

In Room W, he smells the same incense he remembers and walks down the narrow corridor with beaded curtains on either side. Cleopatra and Elizabeth Taylor are still arguing. He tiptoes quietly past them. Across the hall, on the other side of the curtain where Marilyn and Jayne were, there is no one. Many of the compartments are empty. Room W beauties don't just sit around; they have restaurants like Cleopatra does, or own other businesses.

Further down the long corridor, he hears another argument in progress. It's between many women, and the action is fast and furious.

Vivien Leigh is laughing at the others.

"Don't whine to me, Bette Davis. You turned down the role of Scarlett O'Hara, remember? You were cast as another Southern belle in the movie *Jezebel*. The role called for a nasty bitch, and it fit you perfectly, dahling."

"You bet. It fit me a lot better than it would have fit you, you, you Limey. You're from the South? Yeah right, South

Liverpool. Your Southern accent is as phony as your pancake makeup."

Katharine Hepburn interrupts them. "Listen carefully, very carefully. That role was written for me. I demanded an appointment with David O. Selznick. I told him I *am* Scarlett O'Hara."

"Why don't you tell everyone what David said, Miss Prim and Proper," Vivien Leigh counters. "I'll tell you what he said. 'I can't imagine Rhett Butler chasing you for twelve years.' They couldn't hide your ribs, you bag of bones."

"You lie!" Katherine Hepburn and Vivien Leigh pull each other's hair and kick each other.

The women in Room W shout, "Cat fight! Cat fight!" A sizeable crowd of the most gorgeous women Thomas has ever seen are outside shrieking and rooting for their favorite combatant.

"That part should have been mine!" shouts Paulette Goddard, as she enters the fray.

"Horseshit, it should have been mine!" shout Susan Hayward and Lana Turner at the same time.

Jean Arthur, Lucille Ball, Doris Davenport, Joan Bennett, and Tallulah Bankhead join the brawl, punching, kicking, pulling hair, and ripping each other's clothes.

"Mine! Mine! No, mine! Mine, not yours! Mine, up yours!"

For his own safety, Thomas leaves the area as quickly as possible. He notices a stunning woman on the right side of the corridor. She is wearing a tight white satin gown, black stiletto heels, and black pearl necklace. From the back, she seems vaguely familiar. He separates the beaded curtain. When she turns around, she grabs Thomas in a vise grip and carries him bodily out of Room W.

Thomas is crying.

★

Rose carries Thomas like a discarded hamburger wrapper caught in a category five hurricane. She is so strong, he can't offer any resistance.

"Where are we going? Why do you do this to me?"

"Incentive, Thomas, incentive. Enlightenment, Thomas, Enlightenment. That is your number one priority. You are so close, don't blow it now."

"How is getting a little nookie blowing it?"

"When it comes to male-female relationships, you are still a Jerk Being."

"Where are we going?"

"We're here. You have no choice but to walk with me through Room H, Room Hunk."

The fragrances of musk and English Leather fill the air. There are beaded curtains on either side of a long hallway. They pass a compartment with three men who recognize Rose immediately. The men are dressed only in Speedos. They admire themselves in mirrors mounted on all four sides of the Room. They flex their muscles while they slather oil on their bodies to make them glossy and slick.

"Thomas, let me introduce you to three former Mr. Americas. They each won the most important body-building competition in the world. John Grimek, Clarence Ross, and Steve Reeves. Guys, meet Thomas Buchetta. Hi, Stevie."

"Hi, Rose. Is Thomas, a body-builder?"

"No, he's a Jerk Being. Take care, guys, I'm going to show him around."

"Hello, Jacko!" Rose hugs another Hunk. "Thomas, this is Jack LaLanne. He's been with us since January, 2011. Jack started the first health club in the United States."

"Holy Spumoni! Rose, why do you know every one of these guys by their first name?"

"How good of you to ask, Higher Life Form. My answer is simple: familiarity."

"Hi, Johnny. Thomas, please meet Johnny Weissmuller. Both his parents are from Hungary, just like me."

Weissmuller gives Rose a big hug and lifts her off the ground. "Why haven't you been visiting me lately?"

"I've been so busy with Room 214 business. I promise to keep in touch."

"Thomas, Johnny Weissmuller won five Olympic gold medals in swimming, and broke the world's record in each race. He made a bunch of movies and has won all kinds of awards."

"Yeah, great, I'm not impressed. How much talent does it take to walk around in a loincloth with a stupid monkey, while you scream eeeeeeeeeeeeeeeeeya, eeeeeeya!"

"Listen, Higher Life Form, they weren't monkeys, they were chimpanzees, and they can be very hard to handle. When they started filming, the animal trainer told Johnny not so show any fear, or the chimp would attack him. Do you know what he did?"

"No, tell me, I'm completely transfixed and riveted beyond my wildest imaginings."

"He walked up to the chimpanzee, which they named Cheetah, and it bared its teeth and lunged at him. Johnny took his hunting knife out of its sheath and hit the chimp on the side of the head with the knife handle. He put the knife back and held out his arms to pick up Cheetah. It growled once more but quickly stopped. It finally grinned at Johnny, jumped up, and hugged him. He never had any more trouble with the chimp after that."

"That's a heart-rending and moving story. He's a real man, for sure. Tell me, is that the way he treated you on your first date?"

Rose forcibly carries Thomas through the rest of Room H.

"Thomas, this is Jimmy. Hello, Jimmy, how are you?"

James Dean looks up for a brief micro-second from the book he is reading but doesn't say a word.

"He's always so moody. Thomas, have you seen enough?"

"Oh no, how about introducing me to all the dead NFL, NHL, NBA, and MLB players. You must have dated all of them at one time or another."

"Is that so? You know nothing! Here's what I propose. You stay the Hell out of Room W, and I'll stay out of Room H. Is it a deal?"

"It's a deal."

★

At the next Room 214 meeting, Thomas has some interesting news. He munches an onion bagel with cream cheese and chives, and raises his hand to speak.

"So, Thomas, my boy, watcha got for us?" Jehovah asks.

"I discovered something wonderful, but I don't know if it *is* wonderful."

Jehovah laughs. "That reminds me of a joke. This guy is sitting in his office and his boss walks up to him and asks him if he has trouble making decisions. He answers, 'Well, yes and no.' So, what's wonderful?"

"I figured out a way to beam thoughts into Beings in the NetherWorld."

"Holy Pizzoli! Holy Pastrami! Holy Ravioli! You've got to be joshing me!"

"No, really. They will have no idea that the thought-beam is originating from EtherWorld, and the NetherWorld has no way of monitoring us. There's something else."

"What? What?" Jehovah is excited. Sonny and Holy Rollino are so aroused that Their brightness overwhelms Thomas's polarized sunglasses, and he has to close his eyes.

"At the Andromeda Peace Conference, we agreed to send only one message per day into each Human. We put failsafe locks on all receiving equipment, making it impossible for either side to read the other's messages. I figured out a way to bypass the safeguards and listen in on everything they send. I didn't do it, because it would be in direct violation of the rules we agreed to at the Peace Conference."

"Thomas, Thomas, rules are made to be broken. How quickly can you tell me what they are sending?"

"I can have a full printout by tomorrow at fourteen micro-clocks. I will also provide all the technical details about beaming thoughts across the border."

"You get another gold star. Rose, give Thomas some smoked salmon for his bagel. You do like smoked salmon?"

"I love it. As a matter of fact, I'm enjoying the bagels more than the Italian breadsticks. However, I don't see much of a difference between challah and panettone. They are both wonderful sweet breads."

"Thomas, I am truly shocked. There can be no comparison! Challah is as light and delicious as the breath of an angel, speckled with costly saffron, while panettone is fruity, nutty, and heavy as an Italian widow.

"So, who's going to play in Game Week, you wonder?" Jehovah asks. "Everyone except Thomas. He has special work to do. And Rose, of course. She has to watch Thomas to make sure he doesn't shoot himself in the foot," Jehovah says with great joviality.

Thomas returns to his private lab in Room Renaissance. He commutes back and forth from Room Security and his place. He gets his best ideas while studying the heavens with his EtherScope. He remains upset at Rose for placing virtual filters on the lenses. He can faintly see many Swirls in Free Space, but can't get close enough to see anything more than vague shapes of pulsating light. He can only imagine what those pulsations are and fantasizes about being the Director of Swirls. He hadn't known there was such a position until last clock. His virtual peace is broken when he hears a racket coming from the corner of his lab.

Boots and Tabitha are jumping in the air and caterwauling very loudly. They are disturbing Thomas's concentration.

"Shouldn't you go a little easy, Tabitha? You're about to drop kittens."

Boots tells him that they have won the football lottery. This is the very first time a cat has ever won. Back in 1963, a German Shepherd-Poodle mix won, but that's last time a four-legged Being got the best point-spread.

Thomas thinks, *If Boots is so good at figuring out football point-spreads, why can't he figure out mathematical probability of thought patterns?* He places five bar-graph printouts on the kitchen table and asks Boots which of the five will most likely repeat in the next cycle.

Without hesitation, Boots selects printout number three.

20

I feel like Captain Kirk, Thomas muses as he looks through his EtherScope. His father bought him his first telescope when he was ten. When he studied at MIT, he took several astronomy courses and upgraded to a very fine Newtonian Reflector telescope. He used it for many years, and at the time of his death it was still in the back corner of his closet.

He remembers the names of his favorite objects. He programs his EtherScope to view the Planetary Nebula NGC 6302, which looks exactly like a butterfly with blazing colors of chartreuse, bright orange, and true celestial blue.

He turns to the Carina Nebula and views stars as they are being born from a giant primeval womb. *Just like kittens.*

Omega Centauri has 100,000 stars in every color imaginable. The young stars are blue and the oldest are red.

The Galaxy Cluster Abell 370 is so far away it takes the illumination five billion light-years to reach Earth. When Astronomers view Abell 370, they are looking at very old news indeed.

The Sombrero Galaxy is one of Thomas's favorites. It really does look like a Mexican hat, complete with fringe around the edge. Sombrero is so easy to view that he could see it with his first, low-powered telescope. He finds it by referencing the constellation Virgo.

Scientists do not understand everything about the stars, and probably never will. Thomas wishes astronomy were a required course in all high schools throughout the world. He wonders how many Humans stop to think about the wonders of the Universe. *Can you imagine an object so far away that it takes light five billion years to reach Earth?* He speaks out loud. "How many people even bother to look up at the sky at night? Their noses are always straight ahead, pointed at whatever mundane concerns they may have."

Thomas has been doing a whole bunch of serious reading in Room Astronomy. Their library is vast. He figured out how to receive the Hubble Telescope images directly. He can see what Humans see. His EtherScope is tremendously more advanced than the Hubble, but he enjoys looking at the Universe from a Human perspective.

He uses his wide-field lens and turns his EtherScope toward Earth. It really does look like a jewel in a sea of blackness. He can see white lights where there are cities. The east coast of the United States and Europe are lit up like a Great White Way. He can see static electricity charges in the clouds. Thunderstorms are everywhere. The oceans are deep blue, and white angel-shaped clouds float above the continents. The atmosphere is so thin, barely twenty miles high, that the only way to see it at all is to look at the very edge of Earth. If Humans left Earth, it is highly unlikely they would find another planet that could sustain them. There are other life forms, and Thomas has seen them, but they exist on Worlds that could never support Human life. Their atmospheres are different. All their proteins evolved differently.

★

Thomas leaves his observatory and concentrates on intercepting thought-beams. He builds a special Multiplex Q Multiplier and special sampler. With Boots's help, he was able to predict when and where the energy would appear. The NetherWorld code sequence was easy for Boots to decipher. They successfully isolated eight messages and printed them out for Jehovah to see:

Message one – "Life is precious. Children are my greatest legacy. I will go forth and multiply."

Message two – "There is security in having many children to care for you when you're old."

Message three – "Poverty is a state that no Human Being should endure. I must strive to obtain my fair share of the Earth's resources."

Message four – "God does not want me to limit the number of children I have. Any one of them could be a person who changes the world for the better."

Message five – "I'm not being greedy if I provide material abundance for my family. They have the right to the same worldly goods as the people in Europe and America."

Message six – "There is unlimited abundance on Earth. Those who have much are trying to keep me from rising above the poverty level. They want to keep it all for themselves."

Message seven – "Electric cars have no pizzazz. I need a big SUV for my family. I care about their well-being in a hostile world. My job is to keep them safe."

Message eight – "My family deserves the best health-care."

★

Fourteen micro-clocks after the last Room 214 meeting, Thomas attends a special briefing. Most of the EtherWorld is enjoying Game Week, but Thomas and Rose are sitting at the table with Jehovah, Sonny, and Holy Rollino. Thomas presents the eight intercepted messages.

"Your Holiness, Mr. Jehovah, I don't know what they mean. Boots and I figured out how to intercept them. There is no doubt that these messages are genuine, and are being beamed into Humans all over the world."

"Who is Boots? You don't have a woman living with you?"

"He's my cat."

"Your cat! Are you sure he's reliable?"

"Absolutely, Sir. He's one of the best I've ever seen at figuring odds and probabilities. As a matter of fact, he won last week's lottery. You're having dinner with him and Tabitha on Wednesday."

"Who's Tabitha?"

"She's another cat. I guess she's his wife, or his mate, or whatever significant cat-others are called."

"So why didn't you bring Boots to the meeting? He's one smart pussycat. Next time, bring both cats with you. I'll make sure there's some catnip in a small sack, and some kitty tuna."

"They prefer Chicken a la Marsala and enjoy the Sunday *New York Times* crossword puzzle. They do it in ink."

"You don't say, not bad. So, let me read the messages." Jehovah takes a few micro-clocks to study the printouts. He shouts, "Lucy has the unmitigated gall to quote the Bible, from Genesis! Go forth and multiply!" He is furious. "Everyone join hands, right now, do what I say. The combined strength of this Room will show us the way."

"I don't understand," Thomas says. "These messages can't be construed as Evil. How can we object to them?"

Sonny stands up and puts his hand on Jehovah's shoulder. "This is what's going down. Beware of Geeks bearing gifts. At first glance, Beelzie's transmissions *seem* to be positive and of good will. But there is logic in the Universe and in the AfterWorld. There are absolute truths that can't be disputed. One of these is very simple. The EtherWorld is Good, and the NetherWorld is Evil. *Anything* that Beelzie does is for the sake of Evil. There can be no disputing the historical facts. Therefore these messages are Evil."

"I agree with you, Sonny," Jehovah says. "I smelled a rat from the beginning, as soon as Thomas told me that Lucy Pants's messages were decreasing at a predictable rate. The facts indicated it was a calculated plan. Lucy is delusional, as usual. He thinks we can't decipher his motives. I wonder what Freud, Jung, and Adler would make of him? I'm going to ask them to give me a psychological profile of old Lucy Pants. That could help us in future communications. Sonny, what do you think he's after?"

"He knows he can't beat us for control of Human minds by introducing Evil thoughts. He knows he can't spread enough Evil so it rises above the basic Goodness of Human nature. He has chosen the next best thing. Actually, it's what any defeated Evil Supreme Being would do. Since he can't win against us, he will destroy the Earth. It is my omnipotent knowledge that assures me that Beelzie the Bub, Lucy Pants, the Devil, the Great Satan, the Great Republican, no matter what our name for him, intends to destroy the planet Earth."

"What can we do about it?" Jehovah asks.

Sonny suggests all Holy Beings analyze the transmissions. "After we understand their meanings, we will meet again and discuss solutions."

Beelzie's motivation remains unclear. The EtherWorld is having a difficult time formulating an effective strategy.

The meeting breaks up. As Sonny leaves he says, "Verily I say unto you, never accept a gift from Beelzie or from a Republican."

★

Thomas is deep in thought. Rose tries to converse with him, but he answers her monosyllabically. She decides to help him discover the reason behind the NetherWorld transmissions. He has a dozen books on the coffee table in front of his couch. He grabs one and reads.

"Rose, listen to this. Stephen Hawking, the famous scientist says, 'The probability of life spontaneously appearing is so low, that Earth is the only planet in the Galaxy or in the observable Universe in which it has happened.' He goes on to say, 'It is not clear that intelligence has any long-term survival value. Bacteria and other single-cell organisms will live on if all other life on Earth is wiped out by our actions.'"

"That's not a cheery thought, Thomas. I wonder why Humans are in such dire peril?"

"Sheeple are stupid, and blind to their own destruction. Get this. The odds of life appearing spontaneously on Earth are the same as solving a Rubik Cube blindfolded: 50,000,000,000,000,000,000 to 1. It's like throwing four billion pennies in the air, and having them all land heads up. Theoretically it could happen, but it would take trillions upon trillions of years."

"Those SETI antennas have been listening for extraterrestrial radio signals for over thirty years, and so far they have heard nothing," Rose says.

"That's because other civilizations are so far away. By the time they return the signals we transmit, the Earth will no longer exist. There certainly aren't any little green men on Mars, or a voluptuous Goddess colony on Venus. Humans can't hop in a Space shuttle and visit the neighbors. They are *it*."

Thomas has an "aha" moment.

★

Game Week is over, and Sector D once again retains the Jake Trophy by beating Sector C in Bonk. Room 214 is meeting, and there is cannoli and rugelach all over the place.

"Gregorio! How was your vacation?"

"Jovanni! Splendidamente!"

"Thomas, tell Gregorio...er...Jake what you discovered. That is, if you have discovered anything," Jehovah says.

Thomas is very unhappy and tries to control himself, but he gets up from the table and paces back and forth in the Room.

"I don't know what we can do. I don't know what we can do. I'm very bitter, troubled, and fearful for the future. Human Beings are sick. I don't think they were created to survive. They are so self-destructive. They will become extinct due to their own excesses.

"When you have one or two of something, it is indeed important. If you have seven billion of them, they are not nearly as important. What I'm seeing, Your Holinesses, is a terrible tragedy. Each Human life is precious. But seven to ten billion of those lives...." Thomas sorrowfully shakes his head.

"Medical advances have saved millions, and suffering and death from disease has been greatly reduced. We must embrace that as a goodness. But it is a goodness that will help precipitate the ultimate badness, the destruction of the Human race. It's a conundrum that Beelzie is exploiting. When all those saved lives are competing against each other for food and water, Human life will no longer be precious. They will kill each other like rats to survive. I don't know what we can do!" Thomas is waving his arms and raising his voice.

"Beelzie's messages are not negative: Provide for your family, have beautiful children, demand adequate health care, seek out material goods for comfort and safety. His messages are telling Humans in the Third World they are entitled to use as much fuel and energy as do the Americans. If everyone listens to Beelzie, the Earth will cease to exist. That is obviously what he wants."

Sonny comforts Thomas. "There *are* things we can do. Nothing is ever hopeless. Man has free will. That free will gives him choices, not only to choose between Good and Evil, but to make other choices that are either Good for the many, or Good for the few. Humans must choose between Good for their individual selves, or Good for the World.

"What will save Human Beings on Planet Earth is the abandonment of the self, and the reconsideration of the concept of *other*. The planet is more important than any country, or even any family. The task ahead of us is indeed daunting. I'm a fighter, and I like a challenge. Are you up for it?" Sonny gives the staff a pep-talk.

Jake asks Holy Rollino, the Holy Ghostwriter, to assemble the copywriters. They are to hold a special meeting and compose thought-messages to counter those from the NetherWorld.

"This is not going to be an easy task. The thoughts must not be negative. They can't say, for example, that it's wrong to have a large family. What they must do is show how loving it is to reproduce only themselves, without adding to the World's population."

Holy Rollino continues to give guidelines. "We must tell Humans they have the right to clean air and water, and that they deserve to live in uncrowded conditions. The most important single thought we must stress, over and over and over, is that Humans are to think of future generations. What kind of World will their children's children inherit? Now let's get busy."

Thomas is asked to supply technical advice. Jehovah asks Rose to visit Room Head Shrink and get a psychological profile of Lucy Pants. She leaves immediately to complete her assigned task and glides quickly to Room HS.

Freud, Jung, and Adler. *Hey, that sounds like a law firm,* Rose thinks as Sigmund Freud greets her at the door.

"Frieda has the day off, so please, come right in. You are a pretty Being, Miss von Kolisch. Are you married? Do you have sex? Won't you remove your jacket, and lie on zee couch, preferably right next to me."

"No, thank you, Doctor Freud. I prefer to sit in a chair like the one the three of you are sitting on."

"But vee have only three chairs."

"Then I will stand."

There is much whispering and conferring among the psychiatrists. They are shaking their heads negatively. This mini-conference lasts about three minutes. Finally Doctor Adler speaks.

"Rose, vee have decided zat you are a repressed female. Your unwillingness to lie on zee couch, take some of your clothes off, and share stories of your sex life with us, proves, beyond a shadow of a doubt, zat you hate men. Ver you abused as a child?"

"No, I wasn't abused as a child. I was abused as an adult, but that has nothing to do with why I'm here."

"Vas dot sexual abuse zat happened to you as an adult?" Adler asks.

"No, it wasn't sexual abuse. I do not have any problems with sex, at least not *my* problems. I have a friend who's pretty screwed up."

"Vundabar! Tell us about screwed up!" Freud is excited.

"Yes, tell us about getting screwed up," the three doctors say in unison.

It takes Rose several Earth hours to distract the three legendary pioneers of Human psychology away from thinking and talking about sex, to the important reason for her visit.

"Jehovah would like you to do a psychological profile on Lucifer Pants."

"Lucifer Pants! Why didn't you ask us sooner? We have already done it, five Earth years ago. Wait here and I'll get a printout."

Rose glides back to Room Renaissance and says hello to Thomas. Boots and Tabitha are going out the door as she is entering. They are dressed in high fashion. Tabitha is holding a miniature French parasol, and Boots carries an oak English walking stick with a flask on top.

"Where are the two of you going?"

"We are being treated to a gourmet meal by Jehovah, while we watch the Carolina Panthers against the Jacksonville Jaguars. It should be a real cat-fight," Boots says with a smirk.

"Meow," Tabitha says sarcastically. She is annoyed at Boots's corny humor.

"Here's the psychological profile." Rose reads it to Thomas. It has been proofread and copyedited.

"It is hereby stated that this study is medical evidence, and is a full report on the Supreme Being known as Lucifer or Lucy Pants, Satan, Beelzie the Bub, The Devil, Mammon, The Prince of Darkness, The Great Antichrist, The Father of All Lies, The Author of All Sin, The Chairman of the Republican Party, The Great Liar, The Great Murderer, Father of All Contention, The Serpent, Son of Perdition, and by the other countless names that he gives himself, or names he is given by others, be it hereby stated that this psychological study is now complete, and is real and authentic, as presented. Copies are available from Amazon.com for $29.95 and shipping is free. Please allow one week for delivery."

"So, where's the study?" Thomas asks Rose.

"That *is* the entire study. They figured out all the different names Humans use to describe him, but absolutely nothing about his personality. So we're back to square one."

"All you have to do is read Dante's *Divine Comedy*," Thomas says. "The Nine Circles of Hell are concentric, gradually increasing in wickedness. Each sinner is tormented by others in the same circle who will commit the same crimes against him. He will be afflicted in the Inferno, for all eternity, by the major sin he committed.

"The answer to Beelzie's behavior is to look at the Beings in Hell. Study their qualities with great care, and in great detail. He is the sum total of all those traits combined. To predict Beelzie's behavior, we have merely to predict the behavior of any or all of his rotten Eternal Houseguests. Only another Supreme Being who fully knows every facet of Evil can hope to understand what the Supreme Evil Being will do. This is a job for the Holy Quartet."

21

*R*ose glides to Room Renaissance and asks Thomas to accompany her to a meeting in Room 214.

"Before we go, Thomas, let's stop off in Ristoranti Buchetta and get some cannoli. Jake didn't have time."

They glide through the front door. Everyone in Room 214, plus several thousand other guests, is waiting for them and all shout "Surprise!" The Holy Quartet, the staff, and honored guests give Thomas a standing ovation.

Jehovah asks for quiet. "All right, enough already, this is wonderful. Thomas, it's time for you to take off your polarized sunglasses. By unanimous decree, we have decided that you are now an Enlightened Being. We will have our meeting in your restaurant, providing you can bake some decent rugelach."

Thomas doesn't speak. He stands there motionless for several micro-clocks. Suddenly, he does seventeen backward cartwheels at seventeen different oblique angles. Then he takes an expensive Louis XIV wineglass full of Special Reserve California Barbera and shatters it against the fireplace mantle. Holy Rollino shouts, "It's party time!"

The Holy Mandolin Player once again entertains. This time he has an electric mandolin. He joins the musicians in

Room 27, who are set up on a makeshift bandstand in the middle of the floor. There is much dancing and singing.

They push all the tables and chairs aside and clear out a 400-by-500-foot area (it's a big restaurant). The band plays "Hava Nagila," and all the dancers form a circle. They switch to a Tarantella at a much faster tempo, then the band stops cold and plays "Misirlou" at an extremely slow tempo, gradually speeding it up until the entire circle of dancers is spinning so fast they makes a high-pitched humming sound. Humans would see only a blur. Enlightened Beings can dance like this without getting indigestion.

Humans have been dancing in circles since antiquity. Thomas enjoys grabbing hands with Rose and Janis and whirling around in a Spanish Sardana. The band then plays a Thabal Chongba, Moonlight Dance, from Manipur.

By the time the party is half over, they have performed nearly a hundred different circle dances. Enlightened Beings never get tired when dancing, singing, eating, or making love. It's one of the grand perks of the EtherWorld.

After each dance, everyone at the party stomps their feet five times. The shockwave is so fierce, it's felt all the way to Room 213. The last time there was a party like this, Beings in the NetherWorld were so frightened that the entire realm was quiet for nearly ten Earth years.

When the last dance and foot-stomp is finished, the entire group hurrahs. Two thousand Enlightened Beings sitting at the tables hurl their full wineglasses at the stone fireplace.

The sound so frightens Beelzie, he thinks the EtherWorld has invented a new weapon of mass destruction.

"Speech, speech!" Jehovah shouts, pointing at Thomas.

Everyone at the party also chants, "Speech, speech, speech!"

The music stops and the restaurant is quiet. Thomas meekly walks to the bandstand and grabs a microphone.

"Thank you for believing in me. Thank you, Rose, for putting up with me. I know we have much work to do: American Republicans are thriving, the Forbes 400 is getting richer, and the New York Yankees will probably win the playoffs." This gets a laugh from the audience.

"We are Beings of Goodwill and are working for a common purpose. The NetherWorld can't compete with us because they are Evil even towards each other. There is no 'off' switch. Eventually they will destroy themselves.

"All living Beings, past, present, and future, are forever connected in Time and Space. The battle of Good and Evil will continue for eons. Let's make sure we win it."

The party lasts for many Earth days. Ristoranti Buchetta is a total joyous mess. Thomas had his staff take dozens of photographs and intends to mount them over the bar. After closing time, he and Rose sit at a table for two in a corner near the kitchen. The restaurant staff has gone home. Rose has on the same tunic she usually wears to Room 214 meetings, and his imagination fills in all the folds and curves.

"Thomas, come glide with me." She takes him to Room MT, Room Music Teacher. There are a dozen children present. They are learning piano, guitar, and how to write and compose music.

"You are now an Enlightened Being, so you can see and interact with children. Meet your brother, Carlo."

Rose disappears back to her Room. Thomas and Carlo have a tearful reunion. Carlo has chosen to remain an Enlightened Child because his own childhood was cut short on Earth. In time, he will choose to live at another age. Carlo knows everything about Earth that Thomas does, and they decide to beam positive thoughts into their parents to help them in their old age.

He leaves Carlo, and they make plans to play music together. *I wonder where Rose has gone?* Thomas muses as he glides alone in Free Space. He returns to his Room.

Boots greets Thomas at the door, grinning like a Cheshire cat. Tabitha has had five kittens. He tells Thomas he is the proud father of a Siamese, a Burmese, an Abyssinian, a Balinese, and a Persian.

"Boots, how is that possible? You and Tabitha are ordinary pussy cats."

"Oh, isn't that a bit insulting, Thomas? You are hardly a purebred Italian. The Goths, Visigoths, Moors, all manner of Asians and Africans have occupied Italy since recorded history. You probably have some blood in you from every race on Earth. We *ordinary* cats, as you call us, are no different. And besides, Tabitha and I have authored a treatise on feline genetic engineering."

★

There has been one thought gnawing at Thomas. He isn't certain that he's truly Enlightened. He must prove it by the way he reacts to Cindy and Piranha. He picks up his EtherWorld receiver and thought-beam transmitter and glides to the upper atmosphere above Apollo Beach. He tunes in Cindy's cellphone. She's talking to Piranha.

"Listen, Ma, I'm glad you now have a live-in boy toy. I'm not putting you down; I'm in a different place, that's all. I like being alone. I can pick and choose who I want to be with, how long I want to be with him, and I can get rid of him the next day if I want. No more commitments for me, uh uh.

"When I threw Ronald out, he left all Thomas's old shit behind. I never did put it in storage and didn't sort through it after we moved to Florida, but I finally got around to it yesterday. I chucked his old Fender Stratocaster, his saxophone, his telescope, his old jazz records, and his 1940s Lionel trains. I was going to give them to Goodwill, but I didn't feel like dirtying the Lexus. I don't like being reminded of Thomas. His old stuff gave me the creeps."

"Why didn't you have Goodwill come to your house? They pick up. Now you have to pay for trash removal."

"Are you kidding? Not a chance. I'm not having anyone I haven't met before in *my* house. You think they are all goody-goody, and the next thing you know they're casing out your place to rob you. Not me, no way."

"I never thought of that. You're probably right, Cindy. You really can't trust anyone."

Thomas is very angry. His Jerk Being component has been reduced to a mere seven percent, but when he monitors Cindy it rises to sixty-five percent. He finds it only slightly easier to slough off Cindy's comments than before he was Enlightened. He decides to beam down a message directly into her brain. He was going to say something really nasty, like, *"I'm a whore, and I will never be as good a woman as Thomas was a man."* Instead, he decides to send a positive message. Perhaps it will be enough to keep her out of NetherWorld's clutches.

"I have everything I ever wanted, but I really have very little because I don't have myself. I must stop the Pole Dancing School for little girls. That is immoral, disgusting, and wrong. I must also check in on Thomas's parents from time to time to see how they are getting along. Why don't I have a night where I invite people from the homeless shelter

to have dinner for free at my club? It would be good publicity, and it would ease my conscience."

Cindy suddenly has an overwhelming feeling of revulsion, and she cancels the pole-dancing classes. She calls the homeless shelter and offers to provide free meals for their residents every Thursday night.

★

Since Thomas has his thought-beam transmitter working in top form, he decides to glide above New York City, specifically above the United Nations. They are in session, and all the delegates are seated. The Secretary General, Ban Ki-moon, is presiding. Thomas sets the transmitter thought-beam to ScatterShot. After all, Sonny and Jehovah did tell him that rules are made to be broken. The EtherWorld can't wait long enough to beam positive messages into each Human one at a time. He knows that eventually Beelzie will realize that Thomas has broken the conditions of the Peace Conference, and it will probably start another war, but he is willing to take that chance. The war will never really stop. It will just become a convoluted war of copywriters and AfterWorld lawyers.

His thoughts are very clear. *I know we can win this battle. Our messages will be stronger, and Humans will listen. The key is to send ScatterShots into the same group at the same time. The NetherWorld was sending random shots into Humans in many places at once.*

Thomas beams a message into all the delegates at the United Nations.

"My first order of business will be to see that the World's People have enough food and water. They won't have enough if I don't support zero population growth. I must use the United Nations as a forum to spread the word. I will either introduce legislation or support any other excellent measure that makes zero population growth priority one. I will report back to my country that we must take the initiative."

Thomas glides to a position roughly halfway through Sector E. With his newly created technology, he's able to read the thought-waves of Beings across the NetherWorld border in Sector F. He uses the ScatterShot and beams positive thoughts into their minds. He sends a new thought every micro-clock. In an unprecedented move, thousands of Beings cross the border and ask for asylum in the EtherWorld. There are so many crossing that the Composites can't stop them.

Thomas is very happy. Jake names him Director of Resettlement and invites him to be a permanent part of Room 214 Staff. As the newest hire, he will, however, have to take over Janis's duties, including purchasing, inventory, and auditing.

When he hears the news about the defections, Beelzie sits in the corner of his Room and weeps.

★

Without warning, from out of the blackness, Rose ambushes Thomas. She is wearing the tight-fitting white satin gown, black stiletto heels, and black pearl necklace. Although he is Enlightened, he is unable to resist, not that he particularly wants to. Rose has her doctorate and is much stronger. She grabs him and throws him into the passenger seat of his Mustang SlingShot. She drives at 225 warp speed to the edge of the Galaxy and parks the car in Free Space.

"Congratulations, Thomas. You are the first Being in EtherWorld history to be promoted from Universal Awareness to Enlightenment with seven percent Jerk Being still present. But you did it."

"I love you, Rose."

"Well, it took you a long time to get that out. It didn't kill you, did it?"

"I'm already dead, remember? Actually I *was* dead, now I'm not."

"Here's a fact that you haven't paid much attention to, Higher Life Form. Advanced, Good, Enlightened girl-Beings always fall for Bad-boy Jerk Beings. I have loved you ever since we first sat in Room Total Peace."

Rose hands Thomas his Enlightenment Diploma and gives him a sexual hug and a sexual kiss.

"You did it, and now we're going to do it. Thomas, how would you like to go for a Binary Swirl?"

"What's a Binary Swirl?"

"Just the two of us, rolling around."

So Rose and Thomas go Swirling through Space. They do it frontward, backward, sideways, inside out, outside in, him on top, her on top, rolling to the left, rolling to the right, bouncing on the box springs, head to toe, head to head, toe to toe, upside down, downside up, with handcuffs, with black leather boots, with loud jazz, with quiet classical music, using their tongues, their ears, their noses, and their entire feet.

They do it with her taking a flying leap onto him, with him lifting her over his head, with both of them dancing, with both of them swimming, in the shower, on the kitchen table, under the kitchen table, in the Library, in Ray's Pizzeria, wearing masks and costumes, in the back seat of his Ford Mustang SlingShot, on the hood of Janis's Mercedes, on a roller coaster, on a cruise ship, in the middle of Yankee Stadium with everyone watching, on top of the East Bar in Gabriel's Hideaway, in Room Renaissance, in the Andromeda toll booth, just outside of Room 214, 2,000 Earth miles inside NetherWorld, just outside of Room 213 with Beelzie watching, at the Border Patrol station, in Room

PAP, in Room MR, on the Jay Leno show, and in the Reading Room of the American Short Story Writers.

They do it with whips, chains, using a mink glove for massages, with tickling feathers, in a wheelbarrow, balanced in a canoe, on her parents' front porch, in the Oval Office, in the Anal Office, on top of the Statue of Liberty, in a pup tent, in the back seat of a Buick Electra with tinted windows, on the roof, in the basement, using position A, position B, position 69, position 39, with canola oil, with grape jelly, with pumpkin butter, and with chocolate syrup and whipped cream.

They do it hang gliding, with a bump and grind striptease, turning the vibrator all the way up to nine, him placing a mirror on the ceiling, her placing a mirror on the floor, her wearing Frederick's of Hollywood crotchless panties, him taking them off, her wearing a black silk nightgown, him taking it off, her wearing a white satin teddy, him taking it off, him wearing his favorite blue Speedos, her taking them off, her slipping on fishnet stockings and a lace G-string, him taking them off and putting them on himself, him splashing her with Aqua Velva, and her slathering him with Estee Lauder Youth Dew.

They do it in the balcony of the theater, on the beach under the boardwalk, on a bus, in church, on the planet Venus, on the planet Mars, on Queen Elizabeth's throne, with him tying her to a lamppost, with her kissing his tattoos, him kissing her piercings, her biting him, him licking her, them lapping honey out of each other's belly buttons, and them sucking each other's toes.

They do it on a park bench, in a Synagogue in front of the Rabbi and the Cantor, on the subway, in a jet plane, in a teepee, in an igloo, in a thatched hut, in an English cottage, slathered all over with Philadelphia Brand Cottage Cheese. They do it in Philadelphia, in the TWA Building at LaGuardia Airport, on top of a flagpole, in a Macy's dressing room, in the window of Saks Fifth Avenue, in a phone booth, in a photo booth, on a stack of Bibles, and on top of the spread-out Sunday *New York Times*.

They do it on a trampoline, on a rowing machine, in a big brass bed, in a waterbed, on an army cot, in front of Mother Teresa, in front of the Virgin Mary, in front of Pope Pius XII, in a warm hot tub, in a cold mountain stream, with him spanking her, with her spanking him, in a valley meadow, in a hayloft, on her mother's sofa, in a beanbag chair, in a rope hammock, and in a rocking chair.

They do it extremely fast, with lots of screaming and moaning, extremely slow, with gentle tenderness and in silence, with non-stop talking, and with both of them singing Janis's greatest hits at top volume.

In other words, they get to know each other a little better, virtually speaking.

When it's finally over, Thomas asks Rose, "Want to do it again?"

"Sure!"

It's difficult to ascertain how long the Double-Binary Swirl lasted in Earth hours and minutes, probably about two months. They did set a Guinness Book EtherWorld Record for the total number of different positions in a single Swirl, with the same partner. The overall AfterWorld record still belongs to Diphtheria with 11,376 positions, each with a different partner.

★

Cindy has the Tampa Bay Marina outfit her new motor-yacht *Venus and Aphrodite* for a long cruise. The boat is named for her and her mother, and sounds much better than *Cindy and Piranha*. Each letter is painted in gold-gilt with a red border. The fifty-foot luxury craft has two staterooms, a wet bar, and spacious lounge area. She installed special massaging magic fingers in the forward cabin's king-size bed.

Cindy picks up two nice bronze-toned musclemen on Apollo Beach. She is lavished with attention by the men, who get her quite drunk. Unfortunately for her, they are South American drug runners who are intent on stealing her yacht for their smuggling. About twenty miles out of Tampa Bay, they hit her on the head and pitch her into the Gulf of Mexico. A school of barracuda swim around her but don't attack. They recognize one of their own. Two huge sharks, however, do attack, and have Cindy for lunch.

★

"What was that? Where am I?"

Cindy felt a brief second of intense pain and is now dazed and fuzzy. She suddenly sees soft blue and green lights and hears a loud voice.

"Hello, Cindy Esposito!"

"Yes, who are you?"

"My name is Thomas. I'm your Guide, Bitch!"

Joe Randazzo has traveled extensively and writes about what he sees. He believes in the heroism of the ordinary working person, the transformative power of love, and the rejuvenating effects of a truly fine pizza. With his radio station, NX1F, he has contacted many Beings in the EtherWorld, and unfortunately some in the NetherWorld.

His anti-Republicanism is legendary. His OpEd pieces have appeared in many national and local publications, including the *Burlington Free Press*. He will probably be a frequent visitor to Room MuckRaker.

Mr. Randazzo's artwork has been exhibited at venues throughout New England, including Castleton State College, T. W. Wood Art Gallery, and the Helen Day Art Center. He is the author of seven previous books. He lives with his wife Rita in South Burlington, Vermont.

www.ingramcontent.com/pod-product-compliance
Lightning Source LLC
Chambersburg PA
CBHW021044090426
42738CB00006B/180